Fradel's Story

Frances Cohen

&

Marilyn Cohen Shapiro

Fradel's Story

Editor: Mia Crews

Cover photos:
Background vintage postcard: ship departing from Burlington, Vermont on Lake Champlain, New York Library digital collection, created after 1898 date, public domain. From the Cohen family photo collection: Bride and groom-Bill and Frances "Fradel" Cohen; young Fradel on bicycle; Fradel at 6 years old. Back cover: the Cohen kids Laura, Jay, Marilyn and Bobbie with parents Bill and Frances

Cover design by Mia Crews.

See additional photo credits on page 143.

The author may be contacted via email at _shapcomp18@gmail.com_.
www.marilynshapiro.com

ISBN: 9798544981305

This book is dedicated to my siblings,
Laura Appel, Jay Cohen, and Bobbie Chiauzzi

The greatest gift our parents ever gave us was each other.

Author Unknown

Acknowledgements

Thank you to my parents, Fran and Bill Cohen, who were always there for me. Without them there never would have been us. And there never would have been **Fradel's Story.**

Thank you to my siblings, Laura Appel, Jay Cohen, and Bobbie Chiauzzi, who shared our family stories from their perspective. As my dear sister-in-law Leslie Cohen keeps telling us, sometimes it is as if we grew up in four different households!

Thank you to my extended family for filling in the blanks. A special thanks to Arthur Silberstein for co-writing and sharing the biography of his mother and my great aunt, Bea Silberstein. Much of our family's history in Lithuania would have been lost without it.

Thank you to Marsha Helfand Rubenstein and Marty Helfand for sharing the stories of Eli Helfand, my mother's first cousin, my parents' best man, and a lifelong friend of our family.

Thank you to the members of Coburg's writing group, who encouraged my mother to write down her stories for posterity.

Thank you to Laurie and Jim Clevenson of the (Capital Region, New York) *Jewish World* for publishing many of the stories in this book.

Thank you to SOL Writers for encouraging me to publish my articles and books.

Thank you to all my friends and family who offered suggestions on how to improve my writing.

Thank you for the efforts of Mia Crews, my editor, for bringing this project to life.

Thank you to our children, Adam Shapiro and Julie Shapiro and their respective spouses, Sarah Nathan and Sam Massman, who give us so much joy.

Thank you to our granddaughter Sylvie and our grandson Sidney, who light up our lives.

And a special thank you to Larry Shapiro, my husband, my soulmate, my best friend, my muse, and the subject of (too!) many of my past and future articles!

CONTENTS

Introduction

Ever since I could remember, my mother, Frances Cohen, was the family storyteller. Give her an opening, and she would regale any audience with stories of her grandparents' and parents' lives in Russia, her early years of marriage to "My Bill" Cohen, their life in small towns and smaller apartments in the North Country. She told of raising four children, watching them leave for college and for marriage, and their returning with her grandchildren to visit her and my father in their beloved cottage on Lake Champlain.

For many years, these stories were always told orally. Mom shared them when the family got together around the old oak table in the dining room, when she visited friends, and when her children's friends came to visit. What was fascinating was that no one ever got tired of hearing them. As a matter of fact, she was highly regarded as the family historian. If any of her many cousins needed to know who was related to whom and how my father's side was related to my mother's side and what really happened between those two cousins—well, you just had to ask "Fradel," her Jewish name, and the truth would be known.

As my parents got older, my mother realized that she needed to record these stories. We never were one for video cameras and tapes, so she began writing them down on lined paper, usually the five by eight notepads. The writing was messy, with words misspelled and whole sections crossed out, but she began to keep a written history.

My parents retired in 1981 and spent the next nineteen years living six months in Florida and six months in their cottage on Lake Champlain. When it became too difficult to maintain two homes, they sold their cottage to my brother and sister-in-law, and they lived in Florida year-round. When I went to visit, my mother would tell me the stories as I transcribed them onto paper. Unfortunately, these scraps of paper remained in their original state for several years.

In 2006, after a number of health setbacks, my three siblings, our spouses, and I insisted that my parents sell their condo in Florida and move back up north to be closer to the family. Everyone decided that the best location would be close to my husband Larry and me. That May, they moved into Coburg Village, an independent living facility only four miles from our home.

Initially uncertain about leaving Florida, their friends, and their independence, my parents soon realized that this was an ideal living arrangement. Coburg provided to its residents nightly five-course dinners in a lovely dining room, a shuttle service that brought them to grocery stores and doctors' appointments, live entertainment, and numerous activities and clubs.

Soon after moving in, my mother called me to tell me she was joining Coburg's monthly writing group to finally finish all those stories she carried in her head and on those scraps of paper. The night after her first meeting, however, she phoned to tell me she wasn't sure she would fit in.

"Most of them have college educations and write beautifully, Marilyn," she lamented. "They will look down on my family stories as being 'silly and boring.'"

Marilyn and her mother Frances "Fradel" Cohen

However, when she brought her first story to the group the following month, her accounting of why she and my father moved to Coburg, she was surprised to find that the group enjoyed her writing style. "They loved my story, Marilyn!" she told me. "They said I have a real flair for storytelling!" After that, my mother's voice in phone calls after the monthly Wednesday meetings was filled with pride.

Mom rarely had difficulty finding a topic and writing it down with pen on paper. However, the group leader requested that the stories be typed so they could eventually be published in the semi-annual collection and distributed to Coburg residents. My mother asked me to type them. While I was at it, could I, "my daughter the English major," do some proofing and minor revisions so that they would read more smoothly?

Thus began our five-year collaboration. Every month, about a week before the group met, my mother would give me her hand-written story. I would do some editing, including spelling, grammar, and even some tightening of the narrative. Then on Sunday, I would bring over the typed, finished story before we took my parents out for dinner and a drive. If I didn't have it done by Sunday night, the phone calls would begin first thing Monday morning. "Marilyn, if you don't have the time, just bring back my copy," said Mom. "I'll read it from the original." I would assure her that it would be delivered in time for her meeting, even resorting at times to sending the final copy to her via the Coburg fax machine.

Her oral stories evolved into more polished, more complete written documents, always original, always entertaining. She wrote about the Old Country and what it was like for her mother and her siblings to grow up in a small Lithuanian *shtetl* at the turn of the century with the fear of pogroms always on the Jewish population's minds. She wrote about their immigrating to America and establishing their roots for themselves and the first generation of native-born Americans that followed. And she wrote about our family: how she and Bill met on a blind date; how they raised four children in various small towns in the North Country, how they came to buy their cottage on Lake Champlain, how they enjoyed their retirement years. The stories were funny, poignant, sad, and sometimes painful, but they were always ready the first Wednesday of every month for her meeting.

When my father passed away in November 2008, my mother's contribution for December was an open letter to my father. She wrote that she was moving into a smaller apartment down the hall. "Wherever I go, you also go in spirit," she wrote. Grieving quietly, she continued with her life at Coburg, going to the concerts, visiting with friends and family who were always stopping by to see her, and continuing with her writing. All the children asked her to write about our births and early childhood, but she always postponed those stories, focusing on the Old Country, her childhood, her Bill.

On December 22, 2010, my mother had a heart attack. The doctors recommended hospice care and living her remaining time to the fullest. She complied, enjoying visits and calls from the children, grandchildren, her extended family, and the many friends she and my father had made in Coburg and in their lifetimes. She kept writing.

In February 2011, with my sister Laura and me sitting close by, Fran shared her story, "The Birth of My First Child," with her writing group. She described her joy in having a beautiful little girl and her fears that she would not be able to be a good mother. The last words, written in pencil on the bottom, were "To be continued...." She died four weeks later, the day of the club's March meeting.

My parents were not wealthy people and had little of material value: a wedding ring, my Grandmother Ethel's engagement ring, two beautiful, framed pictures of my father at thirteen and my mother at six, a few nice dishes. As my siblings and I sadly dismantled Mom's apartment, my daughter was surprised that I wanted so little. "It's okay, Julie," I said. "We have her stories."

And we do! Her written stories are shared in this book as well as additional stories that we heard and are hopefully recorded in that same beautiful voice. What a gift to her family, her friends, and all who knew and loved this amazing woman!

Marilyn Cohen Shapiro
March 2, 2021
(Tenth Anniversary of my mother's passing)

Part One:

Frances Cohen

Our Roots in Ragola, Lithuania

The Ossovitz family story began in Ragola [also known as Arigala and Ragala] in a *shtetl* (a small Jewish town in Eastern Europe) in the Kovno district in the southeastern section of Lithuania. Ragola consisted of one main cobblestoned street where approximately two dozen families lived. The Lithuanians and Russians—Christians—lived in the outlying district, and most of them were peasants who farmed the land to stay alive. What was left of their crops and livestock they brought to Ragola or other small towns to sell in the marketplace.

Most of the Jewish population of Ragola eked out a living as shopkeepers: bakers, fabric sellers, and a druggist who also served as the town's doctor. Everyone lived very simply on bread, meats, chicken, and lots of herring. They grew their own beans, carrots, and potatoes, which were stored in the winter in a basement covered with sand. Oranges were considered a treat.

The social life of Ragola centered on the synagogue and the *mikvah*, the public bath house. Women and girls usually bathed on Thursday, and the men and boys went on Friday. On Saturday, everyone got dressed in their best clothes and strolled down the main street to attend *Shabbos* (Sabbath) services.

Sunday was the day that all the Christian families came to town to go to church and sell their goods. Those who had no horse and wagon trudged in barefooted, carrying their boots and shoes on their shoulders. When they arrived, they would wipe the mud off their feet and put on their footwear to enter the church.

After church service ended, the town would come alive with activity. The peasants would sell to the Jews additional produce as well as live chickens and ducks which lived in their yards until slaughtered according to Kosher rules for *Shabbos* and other Jewish holiday dinners. In turn, the peasants bought groceries, fabrics, and footwear. On most days—the good days—everyone—the *Yids* (Jews) and the *goyim* (non-Jews)—was happy, got along and looked forward to the next Sunday.

On some days, however, the atmosphere turned dark. Jews lived in fear of violence in the form of spontaneous attacks. The peasants, who spent much of their money at the saloon in town, would get drunk and turn against the Jews, attacking and beating unlucky random targets. Even more frightening were pogroms. Following the commands of government officials or the hateful rhetoric of the town's priest, peasants would attack the Jews, destroying homes and leaving innocent people injured or dead.

Jews were especially fearful in the spring, and one incident brought this fear home. In what was later written up in the world's Jewish papers, a merchant from Ragola (who was related by marriage to my mother's family) was attacked and killed by a group of peasants who believed he had murdered a Christian child to get blood for the *seder*, the ritual celebratory dinner held on the Jewish holiday of Passover. Later it was determined the boy's drunken father had committed the crime.

This is the town—the environment—in which my family originated. My mother Ethel's birth mother Chana's first marriage was to a man whose last name was Buck [first name unknown]. A radical and a "free thinker," Buck and his unorthodox views were too much for the religious Chana and her parents. Soon after the birth of their son Rafael, the marriage was dissolved. A few years later, Chana married Elihu Hirsch Ossovitz. Rafael was soon joined by Sam, his half-brother.

In 1883, Buck came to their home and took Rafael with him to America. Chana, heartbroken, died a few weeks later during childbirth. Chana's parents took Sam into their home and raised him until he emigrated to America. The infant Ethel—my future mother—was placed in a home of a wet nurse.

Three years later, Elihu fell in love with Faigah "Vichna" Levinson, the daughter of a prosperous couple in Ragola. Vichna's father, Meyer Levinson, was a successful grain merchant who earned the moniker Meyer Peterburger as his business took him frequently to the second largest city in Russia. Respected by both Jews and non-Jews alike, Meyer and his wife Nachama operated a prosperous bakery and grocery store from their home. They had five children, a son and four daughters with Vichna the youngest.

Vichna and Elihu were introduced by a matchmaker, as was the custom in those days. At first Vichna's parents did not approve of their twenty-year-old daughter becoming the second wife of a thirty-year-old widower with two children. Their *shidduch* (arranged marriage), however, was a love match, a rarity in those days. Vichna was a beautiful woman, and Elihu had come from a respected family of rabbis. He himself was a scholar, a Hebrew teacher, and a very handsome man. Vichna's parents finally agreed to the marriage. She traveled to Hamburg, Germany for her trousseau, and the Levinsons threw the happy couple a big wedding.

The newlyweds and Ethel shared a shtetl-style "duplex" with the Adlers. Each side of the small wood building held one room with a curtain in the corner hiding a bed to provide the parents some privacy. The two families shared an outhouse. They raised chickens for eggs and, after kosher slaughter, the meat for *Shabbos* (Sabbath) meals.

Vichna warmly accepted Elihu's daughter as her own, and three-year-old Ethel adored her stepmother. In fact, it was not until Ethel was introduced to her maternal grandparents when she was ten years old that she realized that Vichna was not her birth mother. During that visit, Ethel also learned that she had an older brother Sam and a half-brother Rafael in America.

Even though Vichna's parents were well-off, the couple struggled financially. Elihu scratched out a living as a teacher in Ragola. Vichna was the breadwinner, continuing to work in her father's store. In order to better support his family, Elihu made several trips to New York City to teach in a *yeshiva* (Hebrew school). Each time he returned, a baby was born nine months later. The last time, Elihu returned very ill, and his trips to America were over.

By 1900, the couple had four more children sharing their one room house: Joe, Lil, Paul, and Rose. Fearful of the threat of pogroms, Elihu and Vichna hoped to find a way for their oldest daughter Ethel to cross the ocean by herself to *die goldeneh medinah*—the Golden Land—for a better life. That opportunity opened when her brother Sam, who had immigrated to America around1896, sent her money for her passage.

The Pearl Family, Circa 1960

Beginning a New Life in America

At Ellis Island, seventeen-year-old Ethel was met by her brother Sam and her half-brother Rafael Buck, the first time she had actually met either sibling. Sam helped Ethel find a place to live with cousins, and Ethel got a job in an umbrella factory. The following year, her cousin Ella married Louis Leibesman. At the wedding, Sam met Mary Prisman from Baltimore. It was love at first sight, and Sam moved to Baltimore to be with his bride. He started New York Pants with Mary's brother Joseph, a company that grew into a very successful business.

Despite the fact that Elihu had multiple health issues and was very disabled, he and Vichna, had three more children—Bea, Morris, and Ruth—in their tiny home in Ragola. As the oldest girl living home, Lil was given much responsibility for her six younger siblings.

When she was sixteen, Lil was sent to America to join Ethel, who was now living with the newlyweds, Ella and Louis Leibesman. The timing was right. The Leibesmans now had two children, Aaron and Bertha, and Ethel needed to find a new place to live.

As soon as Lil arrived, the two sisters rented a room with a family of six children and four other boarders. In addition to having to cope with the crowded conditions, hygiene was a challenge. The Gibson Girl look—high colored blouses, long skirts, long hair piled under huge hats—was in fashion. Bathing and washing one's hair were a luxury, and washing clothes was done by hand. As my mother recounted many years later, "The good old days weren't so good."

Lil obtained a job as garment worker in a sweatshop in Greenwich Village. She viewed the location—the top floors of the crowded, airless Aisch Building—as "a firetrap." To prevent workers from taking too many breaks or stealing, the owners locked the doors to the stairwells and exits. Despite the poor working conditions, Lil was a fast, efficient worker who was respected by her fellow workers.

When she was 23 years old, Ethel was struggling on her three dollars a week salary working in an umbrella factory. Learning of this, Sam invited her to come and live with his family in Baltimore. At the time Sam, Mary, and their two girls were living with Mary's parents and a single sister Frannie. Considering Sam was never brought up with his sister Ethel, it was wonderful of them have them to take her in and have her live with them for the next several years.

When Paul encountered health problems working in the sweatshops, Lil financed his move to Burlington, Vermont, where he learned the peddling trade from his uncle, Aaron "Archik" Perelman, the husband of Vichna's sister Ittel. First traveling on foot and then on horse and wagon, Paul, later joined by his brother Joe, saved enough money to open a store in Alburgh, Vermont. This was the start of Pearl's, a department store chain that grew to twenty-two stores in Vermont and Upstate New York.

Working in the factory on Washington Place, Lil continued to perfect her skills as a seamstress. When she demanded a raise, she was fired—a blessing in disguise. A week later, on March 25, 1911, the "firetrap"—the Triangle Shirtwaist Factory—was the scene of the deadliest industrial fires in New York City history. A hundred and forty-six garment workers died from fire, smoke inhalation, or falling or jumping to their deaths. The tragedy led to legislation requiring improved factory safety standards and helped spur the growth of the International Ladies' Garment Workers' Union (ILGWU), which fought for better working conditions for sweatshop workers.

In 1910, Elihu passed away, leaving Vichna and the three youngest siblings struggling financially in Ragola. Using her savings, Lil sent $75 to the remaining family to pay for their ship passage. On April 11, 1911, an elegantly dressed Lil greeted her mother Vichna (44), Beatrice (11), Morris (9), and Ruth (6) at Ellis Island. Lil rented an apartment on the Lower East Side of Manhattan for herself, Rose, and the four new immigrants.

If you were wondering why all the Ossovitz family's first names sound so "American," it is because all of the children shed their old-fashioned Yiddish names as quickly as they could once they were arrived in "The Golden Land." Along with going to school, at night, if necessary, to learn English and work toward citizenship, they all changed their Yiddish names to ones that reflected their new lives. *Schalama* became Sam; *Ettel,* Ethel; *Yossel,* Joseph; *Pesach,* Paul; *Shira Lea,* Lil; *Rochel,* Rose; *Peshka,* Beatrice/Bea; *Moisha,* Morris; and *Chona,* Ruth. Even their mother Vichna went by "Fanny" outside the home. My Aunt Bea recalled years later her embarrassment when her mother called her *Peshka* in front of her American friends. As a matter of fact, I didn't know most of their Yiddish names until Aunt Bea recounted them in the memoir she wrote at 91 years old!

Lil continued to be the main breadwinner in the family. She obtained promotions as a seamstress in various factories specializing in blouses and dresses. She often made as much as $20 a week, a greater salary than most of the married men with whom she worked. Her hard work came with sacrifices. Lil attended night school, but after a long day in the shop, she often fell asleep in class. As a result, she never spoke or wrote English proficiently, relying heavily on *Yiddish,* the language used by Jewish people in central and eastern Europe before the Holocaust, her whole life.

Now that the entire Ossovitz family was in America, Vichna focused her efforts on making sure that her all of her children were married and settled. She first turned her attention to Ethel, 27, unmarried and living in Baltimore. Through her cabbage soup and matchmaking, she saw the stepchild she had raised since "Ettel" was three, was happily settled with Joseph Cohen, a fellow *landsleit.* Lil married Sam Waldman, a butcher, and worked alongside her husband in stores in New York City, St. Regis Falls, New York, and for most of their lives in the Syracuse area. The two brothers in Burlington found wives: Joe married Leona, and Paul married seventeen-year-old Bertha Leibesman, the second cousin born the year Lil came to America. Bea married Sol Silberstein, her high school sweetheart and an accountant, and they eventually settled in Brighton Beach in Brooklyn, New York. Rose married Ruby Helfand, who eventually opened his own store, which he called "Ruby's," in Brushton, New York. Morris married Dorothy "Dot" Harris and, with Paul's help, opened up their own store in Chateauguay, New York. Ruth married Isidore Kropsky, settled in Burlington and after managing a Pearl's for several years, established their own business.

The entire family remained close throughout their lives, including the 23 children and many descendants of the original nine siblings from Ragola, Lithuania. And all of us recognize and appreciate the strong role our Aunt Lil played in our history.

The Pearl family with their spouses

Pearl's Department Store

The story of Pearl's Department Store is a very interesting one as it involves so many of my mother's family, the Pearls.

Let's start at the beginning. Uncle Paul, my mother's twenty-year-old brother, was living on the lower East Side in New York City with his family in a crowded flat. With very little education and a short, skinny build, he was only able to get a job in a sweatshop making $7 a week. After seeing a doctor for a persistent cough, Paul was diagnosed with consumption, a direct result of poor working conditions and a poor diet. It was suggested that he leave the city.

My grandmother Vichna had a sister Ittel, and she, her husband Archik Perelman, and their family lived in Burlington Vermont. Lil encouraged him to pay them a visit. Paul liked the North Country, and his health improved in the country air near Lake Champlain. With Lil's financial support, Paul started in the peddling business, learning the trade from Archik and initially following his routes.

Paul went door to door with a pack on his back peddling his wares throughout Vermont and Upstate New York. He soon expanded the business so that it would not compete with Archik's territory. After saving enough money, Paul managed to get a horse and wagon. Since he was doing well, he asked his brother Joe to join him in his rounds.

As the two brothers peddled their way through Vermont, they realized that the farmers and families to whom they sold merchandise found it difficult to pronounce their last name, which was Ossovitz. The customers, who knew Paul and Joe as the nephews of the peddler Archik Perelman from Burlington, Vermont, referred the two of them as the "Perelman Boys." For simplicity's sake, my uncles gave their last name as Perelman.

A year after they started their partnership, Uncle Paul and Uncle Joe decided to open a store in the small village of Alburgh, Vermont. They bought a piece of land with a barn on it. While the store with its second-floor apartment was being built, Paul and Joe slept in the barn with the horse and wagon. Many years later, Paul related to me that they didn't need an alarm clock as the horse would wake them. Simplifying their name even more, Paul and Joe named the new store "Pearl's Department Store," and the family legacy began. Three of the brothers, Joe, Paul, and Morris, eventually legally changed their name to Pearl. Sam, the oldest, was the only brother to keep the surname Ossovitz. Thereafter, however, all the relatives identified themselves as part of "the Pearl family."

Paul and Joe soon established a second store in Swanton, Vermont. When war was declared in 1917, Uncle Paul was drafted into the Navy. Joe ran the store while Paul served his country. When the war was over, Paul was happy to come back to Alburgh. Soon after Paul's return, Joe announced that he and his wife Leona wanted to go back to New York City.

In 1923, Paul married Bertha Leibesman, the second cousin born the year Lil came to America. They lived in the apartment over the store. "Birdie," as she was known by her family, was very bright and was a big help in making Pearl's Department Store a success. Within a few years, they were owners of a chain of twenty-two stores in upstate New York and in Vermont. They became very wealthy, the most successful of the nine Ossovitz children.

In the 1930s, the country was in the midst of The Great Depression. Many members of the family needed help, and Uncle Paul was in a position to do so. Uncle Paul's philosophy was, "Helping someone with a handout only helps them temporarily. It's more important to give a man a job."

Over the years, many family members came to work for Pearl's Department Store. Six of his siblings and/or their husbands worked for the chain, as did fourteen of the grandchildren. My husband Bill and I were one of the first grandchildren to work for Uncle Paul. Uncle Joe and his family also moved back up from New York City and resumed management of the Swanton, Vermont, store.

Pearl's Department Store, Keeseville, New York, circa 1960

14

All the stores were successful. The people in these small villages loved to shop at Pearl's. The managers and their staff were friendly, and the store carried clothing and a great deal of other useful merchandise at prices the average family could afford. Stores were scattered throughout Vermont and New York. The central store and warehouse were in Glens Falls and were eventually run by Paul's son Elliot and his family.

By the 1960s most of my aunts and uncles had retired.Most of the grandchildren had left Pearl's to open their own businesses, and local people continued managing the stores. When Paul died in the 1990s, his son Elliot took over the management of the stores.

Time brings many changes. By the 1970s, many superhighways were completed, including the Northway. The small towns became bedroom communities. It brought an end to the small-town, family-owned stores. People now preferred to travel on the superhighways and shop in big malls.

The last Pearl's Department Store went out of business in 1983, seventy years after who once was known as Pesach Israel Ossovitz had first started peddling with a pack on his back. But the Pearl family will always be grateful to our Uncle Paul for his setting up businesses for so many and supporting many others when they opened their own stores.

My Parents' Romance

They say that all marriages are made in heaven. My parents also had help from my grandmother Faigah "Vichna" Ossovitz.

My mother Ethel was the oldest daughter of nine children, who all eventually immigrated to the United States from a small hamlet called Ragola, which was part of Lithuania.

Joining the wave of Jewish immigrants who came to the United States at that time, Ethel, only seventeen years old, arrived at Ellis Island in 1900. It was the era of horse and buggy, and William McKinley was president of the United States. It was quite an ordeal for a child to leave her parents, cross an ocean by steerage, and then find a way to support herself. But with the help of her older brother Sam, who had come to America a few years earlier, Ethel settled in New York City, got a job, and lived with different relatives.

Two years after Ethel arrived in America, Ethel's older brother Sam married and moved to Baltimore. My mother was really struggling, as she worked in a factory making umbrellas for only three dollars a week. Her brother and his wife Mary generously invited her to come and live with them in Baltimore. While Ethel was living in Baltimore, four more of her siblings arrived in the United States.

In 1910, Ethel's father Elihu passed away. Lil sent the $75 needed to pay for steerage and fees for the now-widowed Vichna and the three youngest children. The four of them settled in the Lower East Side of Manhattan.

Now that the entire Ossovitz family was in America, Vichna now focused her efforts on making sure that her oldest daughter Ethel, who was 27, was married. Every Sunday all the *landsleit* (friends from the old country) would congregate at the Ossovitz's. Since there was little money, Vichna would make a big pot of cabbage soup and homemade bread and serve it with lots of herring. One Sunday Joseph Cohen, a lonely tailor, came to visit. He had come to America when he was 17 from the same town as the Ossovitz family. He told Vichna that he had a job in a children's coat factory making $13 week. He was sleeping on a cot in his sister's apartment. Vichna said, "What you need is a wife, and I have just the girl for you—my Ettel."

The problem was that Ethel was living in Baltimore. That situation was soon resolved when Joseph courted Ethel by writing letters and traveling the

Joseph Cohen

Ethel Ossovitz Cohen

long way to visit. Ethel eventually returned to New York City to live with her stepmother.

Vichna's matchmaking skills proved to be successful as their romance continued to bloom. Every Sunday, Joseph came to visit to see Ethel and to feast on Vichna's cabbage soup and other goodies. Joseph bought Ethel a warm winter coat and other presents. (Later I would tease my mother that she was a kept woman!).

After courting her for several months, Joseph took Ethel to the jeweler, and they picked out a diamond engagement ring. Wanting to make sure the price offered was fair, Joseph left Ethel for security so he could have the ring appraised. He returned an hour later and purchased the ring for $100, which would be over $2600 today!

Soon after they were engaged, Joe sent Ethel, dressed in the new coat he had bought for her, to a resort in the Catskills for two weeks for vacation by herself. As my mother later told me, "In 1911 you did not go on a vacation with your bride to be!"

Soon, Vichna was busy arranging a big wedding for her Ethel. On January 14, 1912, one of the coldest nights of the year, Ethel and Joe were married in a large banquet hall filled with family and friends from Ragola. Each guest paid twenty-five cents for the hat check, which covered room rental and a keg of beer. Vichna and all the guests prepared the wedding meal. Their wedding gifts consisted of pillows, blankets, pots and pans, dishes, candlesticks, an ironing board, and an iron. Guests included the Adlers, Vichna and Elihu's shtetl-mates in Ragola, a friendship that was retained for many, many years. In fact, the members of the Adler family were at Ethel and Joseph's fiftieth anniversary celebration.

The newlyweds moved into a three-room apartment on Houston Street, where they paid $8 a month rent. The first week of their marriage, Ethel, the bride, made a pot of cabbage soup. My father said, "Ethel, please do not make cabbage soup. I am tired of cabbage soup. I don't even *like* cabbage soup!" My mother replied, "You always thanked my mother for her delicious soup." My father replied, "It was the proper thing to do. I didn't like the soup! It was my way of saying thank you for giving me a lovely bride!"

Nine months and four days after the wedding, their son Eli—named after Elihu—was born. Five years later, on September 1, 1917, they welcomed me into the world. While my mother was still in the hospital, my father wrote my official name as Frances Cohen on my birth certificate. At home, however, I was always their "Fradel." My given name was obviously very popular that year. By the time I entered high school, I added "Evelyn" as my middle name to differentiate me from all the other Frances Cohens in my class.

Ethel's brother Sam and his wife Mary continued to be wonderful to my folks. Every summer after Sam's visits to New York, a big package would arrive at my parent's apartment, filled with sheets, towels, and other household goods. During the Great Depression, Sam sent rent money to help Ethel and Joe.

My parents shared over fifty-four wonderful years together until my mother passed away in 1966 at the age of 82. Bereft, my father left New York City and came north to live with my family in Keeseville until he joined his beloved Ethel in 1968.

After Ethel passed away, my father gave me my mother's engagement ring. I wear the ring every day and cherish it very much.

Aunt Rose and Uncle Ruby

I'm so lucky that my mother had lots of siblings. I was surrounded with lots of loving aunts, uncles, and cousins. Of all the relatives, I was closest to my Aunt Rose, Uncle Ruby, and their older son Elliot.

My first memories of my Aunt Rose were when I was very young as she spent a great deal of time with me. She made clothes for me and even sewed some of the clothes for my trousseau. After Bill and I were married, Aunt Rose taught me how to cook. As the mother of two sons, she treated me as the daughter she never had.

Aunt Rose and Uncle Ruby had a wonderful marriage that lasted almost a half a century. They met under very romantic circumstances. Rose worked in New York City in a factory. One rainy day, she was walking home from work and went into a restaurant on Delancey Street to get out of the downpour. As fate may have it, Uncle Ruby was her waiter. Visiting over coffee, Ruby told the poor girl, who was drenched and disheveled, that he was to be finished very soon for the day. Since he had an umbrella, he would be glad to walk her to her home, which was just across the near-by Williamsburg bridge.

When Aunt Rose arrived home, her mother saw how infatuated Aunt Rose was with this tall, handsome guy. Her mother invited Ruby to stay for dinner. That first dinner led to many other dinners. Vichna, ready to feed everyone, would serve herring, boiled potatoes with sauerkraut, and homemade cake and challah. The romance flourished, and they were married within the year.

Soon after they were married, Uncle Ruby lost his job as a waiter. It was the Great Depression, and restaurants did not need as much help. Aunt Rose and Uncle Ruby moved up north to join the family in working at one of the many Pearl's Department Stores. Ruby eventually opened his own store, Ruby's, in Brushton, New York.

Aunt Rose and Uncle Ruby

Everyone loved Ruby as he had a wonderful sense of humor. When one of his customers complained that the underpants she bought at his store had holes in them, Ruby said that those were for ventilation. Uncle Ruby hated the Yankees, and he rarely missed their game on the radio just to cheer on the opposite team. At family get-togethers in our home in Keeseville, he would often sneak out to his car, turn on the radio, chew on Chiclets gum, and curse out "those damn Yankees!"

Aunt Rose and Uncle Ruby lived happily in Upstate New York and, although the only Jews in the town, were beloved by everyone. When Aunt Rose died just before their planned fiftieth anniversary party, her funeral was held in Burlington, Vermont. Even though that was 100 miles from their hometown, all the stores in Brushton were closed for the day so that everyone, including the local priest and the minister with his family, could attend the funeral,

Ruby missed his Rose. When he got lonesome, he would put a sign in the window of his store that stated, "Closed for Jewish Holidays" and travel to visit his children and grandchildren.

Ruby lived until he was ninety years old. His funeral, which was held in Burlington, Vermont, was also hugely attended as he was beloved by all the family and the many friends he and Rose had made during their lifetimes. During his eulogy, the rabbi said, "Ruby was not a religious man, but he took more time off for the Jewish holidays than anyone else I ever knew."

As I mentioned before, Ruby and Rose had two sons, Elliot and Sol. I was especially close to their elder son, Elliot. When things were bad during the Depression, Elliot would spend the summers with my family in New York City. I'm forever grateful to him for introducing me to my husband. Elliot was best man at our wedding, and he drove the car that we took from New York City up north after our honeymoon. It an unforgettable trip. I sat in the front seat with Elliot and Aunt Rose. Bill sat in the back seat with all the wedding presents, including a floor lamp that Bill had to hold for the eight hours. As adults, we remained very close and have spent much time together in Florida and up north. Elliot and his wife Florence were at our fiftieth wedding anniversary. After Florence passed away, Elliot remarried. We have remained very close to Elliot and his second wife Marty. In May

2010, I went down to Staten Island to celebrate his daughter's sixtieth birthday. I sat with Elliot and visited as if we were still children.

I am very grateful for our relationship with Ruby, Rose, and their family. They very much enriched Bill's and my life.

Growing Up in Coney Island

I spent most of my early childhood in Coney Island. I loved living in that special section in the New York City borough of Brooklyn, especially during the summer.

We did not have many of the conveniences that we have today. Rather than a refrigerator, we had an icebox. The iceman delivered ice every other day. We had a pan under the ice box. When we forgot to empty the pan, there would be a huge puddle on the floor. There were no supermarkets, just local grocers. Milk, which was not homogenized, was purchased from the grocer. It was stored in large metal buckets and ladled out. As the ladle was often left out with the milk uncovered, flies and roaches swarmed around the bucket. Mice licked the ladle until they were chased away by the store's

resident cat. When we brought the milk home, the cream was on the top, and my mother would make whipped cream with a hand beater. I grew up before radios, washing machines, dryers, and dishwashers. Even toilet paper was yet to be invented. We used orange wrappers and pages from the Sears catalog.

I lived two blocks from the beach and the boardwalk. I loved to go swimming in the ocean and walking the boardwalk. We had two big amusement parks within walking distance, Luna Park and Steeplechase. I preferred Luna Park as it had a circus. It was such fun watching the clowns, the animals, and especially the men and women on the trapeze. Nearby was the famous Nathan's hot dog stand, where we could buy a hot dog with sauerkraut for five cents.

As there were no televisions, we went to the movies every Saturday. For ten cents, we saw a double feature along with newsreels, a serial, and cartoons. We bought a penny's worth of candy and enjoyed the entertainment. On rainy days, we stayed indoors, drawing pictures with crayons and reading books from the library. We did not have as many toys as our grandchildren and great grandchildren have today, so we improvised. My brother made a train out of drawers from my father's Singer sewing machine.

As all little girls, I loved to play with dolls. My mother had bought me a small celluloid doll with moving arms and feet that I could even bathe. I wanted a new doll carriage, but we were in the midst of the Great Depression, and my parents could not afford to buy me one from the store. So, we became creative. A shoebox became my doll carriage. My mother made a hole at the end of the shoebox and put a string through it so I could pull the carriage. The top of the box became the hood. She also gave me scraps of material which I made into a pillow, a carriage cover, and clothing for my doll. With a child's imagination, I thought that my doll and doll carriage were the most beautiful in the world.

It was convenient to live near the beach, but my neighborhood was not the best. It was all pavement—no flowers and no lawns. One summer, my second-grade teacher thought it would be a good summer project to learn how things grow. The last week of school, she had us bring in a small wooden cheese box and a small potato. She helped us put the dirt that she supplied into the bottom of the box. We cut up the potato, placed it in the dirt, and then covered the potato with more dirt. I placed the potato plant on the fire escape and watered it every day. In July, I was happy to see some green leaves. My parents and teacher had never told me that potatoes grow underground. So, when August arrived, I got so angry that no potatoes had grown on the leaves, I just dumped the plant. I was so surprised to find four little potatoes!

Looking back, I had a very happy childhood. Although we did not have much money, I never felt deprived!

Zayde

I was around four years old when *Zayde* (Jewish for Grandpa) came to live with my parents, my brother Eli, and me.

Life had been difficult for my Zayde. His first wife died giving birth to my father Joseph. When she died, she also left a beautiful red-haired five-year-old daughter Becky. Zayde could not raise two young children alone. Shortly after his beloved wife died, he remarried as he needed someone to take care of the children. His new wife was cruel to the children, and he divorced her. He remarried a third time to a woman who raised the children as her own.

When Becky was twenty years old, Zayde brought Becky to America. He arranged with a matchmaker to get her a husband, and then he returned to Europe. Soon after, when my father was fifteen years old, Zayde sent him to America to live with Becky and her husband Louis. My father worked in the garment district as a tailor, married Ethel Ossovitz, my mother, and had two children, Eli and me.

Fradel and brother Eli

In 1921, the war had ended in Europe, and the Germans had destroyed their village of Ragola in Lithuania. Zayde wanted to leave to come to America to be with his grown children, and he begged his third wife to leave. She didn't want to go, so Zayde came to America alone. He sent money to her for the rest of his life but could never persuade her to come to New York.

When Zayde arrived in New York, my parents, my brother Eli, and I were living in a crowded three-room apartment. We shared a bathroom with four people in the next apartment. Soon Zayde began giving Hebrew lessons, and he was able to contribute to the household.

Despite the further crowding, I loved having my Zayde living with us. As soon as Zayde arrived, we became very close. He adored me, and I loved him. He kept telling me that I reminded him of his first wife, the love of his life.

Zayde soon found out what the rest of the family knew: Becky's marriage was not a happy one. Becky had had several miscarriages, but she and her husband Louis never were able to have any children. Louis blamed Becky and treated her terribly. Louis was also a show-off. They had a nice apartment and dressed nicely, but he never gave Becky enough money for food. He said, "The stomach has no windows. No one can tell what you eat."

Zayde and my parents felt very sorry for Becky. Besides having no children and a bad marriage, Becky felt guilty that her husband would not let Zayde live with them even though they had a larger apartment than my parents did. Louis was so selfish that he would not even allow Becky to have her father over for dinner. Becky's only option was to visit us to see her father.

When I was eight years old, Zayde took me to the Bowery Saving Bank and opened a trust fund for me with $700 he had saved for this purpose. He told me, "A girl has to have a dowry." Here was an immigrant who could not speak English but was very smart.

Four years later, in 1929, my Zayde died. I was devastated, and I couldn't stop crying. My Aunt Bea, my mother's sister, set me straight. "I know how much you loved your grandfather. However, he was an old man and very sick. He was very frail and almost blind. Your mother had to take care of him around the clock. It was a blessing for him and your mother that he passed away." I accepted his death but never forgot how good he was to me, his *shayna klayna maidelah* (beautiful little girl).

After Zayde passed away, my mother and father kept in touch with Becky and continued to invite her to our home. My mother once sent me to visit Becky while Louis was not home. Unfortunately, he caught me just as I was leaving and yelled loudly at me to not return. I never went back to their apartment again.

When I was married in 1940, I took $500 out of the trust fund my Zayde had established for me and purchased furniture for our first apartment, including a maple bedroom set and maple furniture for our living and dining rooms. A few years later, the remaining money was used as the down payment on our first house.

My Zayde's legacy lives on through his great-grandchildren. All of the children have at least one of the pieces of furniture we purchased with my Zayde's trust fund in their home. The maple bedroom set, which moved with us our entire marriage, eventually settled in our bedroom in our cottage in Lake Champlain. My son Jay and his wife Leslie, who purchased the cottage in 2000, now have the set.

And Becky? Louis died two years before Becky, and at that time it was found that he had a condition that had resulted in his wife's inability to carry her pregnancies to full term. After all those years of abusing my poor aunt, he was the one who was to blame. Two years later, my aunt died of cancer and medical problems created by the multiple miscarriages. My only regret is that I did not spend more time with Becky.

Thanksgivings Past and Present

The way that I have celebrated Thanksgiving has changed over the years, but it always has been a special holiday for my family and me.

Of all the Thanksgiving dinners, my first one when I was seven years old was one of the most memorable and unforgettable. My mother had invited my two aunts and their families to share a Thanksgiving dinner at our house. During the weeks before Thanksgiving, our teachers at school kept telling us the story of The First Thanksgiving. They related how the Pilgrims landed on Plymouth Rock; how they survived their first winter with the help of the Indians; and how one fall day the Pilgrims invited the Indians to a huge celebratory dinner with turkey and all the trimmings.

My two cousins Elliot and Sol, my brother Eli, and I told our mothers that we would like to have turkey on Thanksgiving as the Pilgrims did. In 1921, however, turkey was not plentiful and was very expensive. Therefore, so as not to disappoint us, my mother and aunts plotted to serve chicken but tell the children it was turkey.

Thanksgiving Day arrived. All the family was sitting around the dining room table. My Aunt Rose cheerfully walked in from the kitchen with a huge platter of cut-up chicken and announced, "Here comes the turkey!"

Immediately my Uncle Ruby protested. "Rose, why did you make turkey?" he said. "It's so expensive, and I don't even like it!" My aunt, ever the diplomat, called my uncle into the kitchen and did some quick and quiet explaining. Meanwhile, my cousins and I enjoyed eating the 'turkey' and remarked throughout the meal how delicious it was and how much it tasted like chicken but better.

It wasn't until many years later when I was married and was invited to my Aunt Rose and Uncle Ruby's house for a turkey dinner that they finally told us the story about our first Thanksgiving with the *shvindl* (fake) turkey.

As I grew older, I enjoyed Thanksgiving holidays the most when my children and grandchildren visited. The Thanksgiving holiday became a Thanksgiving Family Reunion. Thursday was turkey with Mom's Favorite Stuffing (my specialty) served on our huge turkey platter and all the trimmings; Friday was leftover turkey sandwiches, and Saturday was turkey soup. As the family grew and spread, the location of the reunion may have changed, but the celebration was the same. The turkey was always served on the same colorful platter that was carted from home to home.

When Bill and I moved to Florida, Thanksgiving was very different. We celebrated the holiday like most of the other senior citizens: We went with neighbors to an early bird special at 4:30 p.m. as we did not like to drive back to our condominium in the dark. But Bill and I missed being with our family.

Now that we are back up north, this Thanksgiving will be much more meaningful. We will be having Thanksgiving with our children and other close family, complete with real turkey (no chicken in disguise) on our turkey platter and all the trimmings. And for this we are very thankful.

Bill's Parents: Annie and Joseph Cohen

My husband Bill's father Joseph Cohen was born around 1885 in Minsk, Russia. When he was thirteen, he was drafted into the Russian army, where he played a trumpet in the military band. When the Russo-Japanese War broke out, he decided that he needed to leave Russia for America.

According to family legend, Joseph escaped across the Russian border in a hay wagon. At one point, guards stopped the wagon and thrust bayonets to find any refugees. If the person was found, the hay wagon was set on fire. Even though his shirt was torn, he was not found. He spent a year in England to learn the language and then went back to Germany to take the boat to America.

When the 20-year-old immigrant arrived in Ellis Island in 1905, he gave the officials his given name, Yussel Zabalevich. As his last name was nearly impossible to pronounce, he was asked from which "tribe" his family was associated. Let me explain: In the Jewish religion, everyone is part of one of the three major tribes based on their role in ancient society. Most Jews trace their roots to what is known as *Israelites,* who are the "common" people. A smaller percentage are identified as *Levites*, who were priests' helpers in the First and Second Temples. The last, smallest group are identified as the *Kohanim* or the priests. The immigration officers used this delineation to help shorten, simplify, or even completely change the difficult surnames to more Americanized versions. The Israelites' names were often translated into the name of their occupation in the Old Country, such as Carpenter or Shoemaker, or the English translation of their actual name, like Green or Black. The Levites became Levy, Levitt, or Levites. The *Kohanim* were given last names like Cohen, Cowen, Kohane, or Kahn.

My father-in-law was a *Kohanim*. He may have walked into Ellis Island Yussel Zabalevich, but he walked out as Joseph Cohen. Joseph moved in with a sister and took a job as a motion picture operator.

Grandma Annie, Bill's mother, was born in 1891 in Burlington, Vermont. She was the second child of Isaac "Itsik" and Sarah Rivkah Perelman, who had immigrated to the United States with their son Moe two years earlier from a small hamlet in Lithuania. Her parents were the second Jewish family to arrive in Burlington. Isaac started out managing a second-hand antique store. Grandma Annie's baby carriage originally belonged to President Calvin Coolidge when he was a baby. Although Issac did not speak English well, within a few years he became quite successful and owned a great deal of property.

By the time Annie was in third grade, there were four more siblings at home. Annie did not do well in school as she had poor vision and an undiagnosed hearing problem. Her parents took her out of school to help take care of the other children. She spent the rest of her childhood as the caretaker of her family and siblings. She recalled in later years that her younger sister Jen was beautiful and a talented singer, and Annie often listened to her playing the piano for suitors while she was working in the kitchen. While Annie cooked and cleaned and took care of the home, her brothers and sisters completed high school, and the brothers completed college.

It was unfortunate that the oldest child did not have the advantage of the education her younger siblings had. Although her parents and siblings did not recognize it, Annie was a very bright individual. She never owned an address book as she had a photographic memory and remembered everyone's address and phone number. She remembered all the recipes for her wonderful food.

*Joe and Annie Cohen
with daughter Pearl*

When she was twenty-two years old, her oldest brother Moe and his wife Bess, who were living in New York City, urged her to come to visit. They wanted to introduce her to their neighbor Yussel Zabalevich A.K.A. Joseph Cohen. She accepted their invitation. The romance flourished, and they were married within a year; on February 13, 1913. Wilfred (Bill) Cohen was born a little less than one year later on February 7, 1914. He was followed by Pearl, who was born in January 1917, and Nesbith (Nesh), who was born in June 1923.

Bill's father was very ambitious and worked long hours in the penny arcade business. He loved what he did and even invented some of the attractions, including the fortune teller. As this was before patents, Joseph never received credit. A mechanic, Joseph later was working part-time as a motion picture machine operator for a man named Adolph Zukor. One day Zukor informed Joe that he and a group of men were leaving New York City to go to a place called Hollywood, California, to make motion pictures. He asked Joseph to join them as there was a need for a good motion picture operator. Joseph replied, "Motion pictures are a fad. Penny arcades are here to stay." He remained in New York City. Zukor went to Hollywood and was one of the three founders of the highly successful Paramount Pictures.

Unfortunately, when the banks failed in 1929, so did Joe's business. These were difficult times for the family. Joe continued to work for others in the penny arcade. Annie baked and sold carrot cakes and date and nut breads to supplement their income. Despite all these hardships, Annie and Joe had a wonderful thirty-five-year marriage and a loving relationship.

When Bill and I met in 1939, I got to know my future in-laws through visits to their home while we were dating. After World War II began, Pearl's husband Danny Eichler was drafted. Pearl moved in with her parents. When Danny returned home in 1945, the four of them continued to live together. Joseph, who was a heavy smoker, was in failing health. He died in 1948 of lung cancer, a few months before our son Jay was born. Jay is named after his paternal grandfather.

By this time, Bill and I were living in Potsdam, New York. Despite the fact that we lived up north, 350 miles away, I had an unusually close and loving relationship with my mother-in-law. She was always there for me. When I arrived home from the hospital after each new baby, she came with a small suitcase but lots of energy and took care of me. On other occasions, whenever she was needed, she was just a phone call away.

Once we moved to Keeseville, Grandma Annie loved to visit us in the summer to escape the city's heat and to spend time at the beach in Port Douglas on Lake Champlain. She said it was her vacation. Since she loved to shop and cook, she took over the kitchen, so it was really *my* vacation.

Grandma Annie was not only there for us but also for others in the community. She was very active in many charitable organizations. When she passed away, the *New York Times* had a long obituary listing all the organization and good work she had accomplished in her lifetime. We are thankful to both Grandpa Joe and Grandma Annie for enriching our lives.

Bill Cohen

Today is February 7, 2007, so I want to write about a very important man in all of our lives, your father, grandfather, and my true love, Bill.

Wilfred "Bill" Cohen was born on February 7, 1914, the first child of Joseph and Annie Cohen. He grew up in Brownsville, New York, which is a residential neighborhood located in eastern Brooklyn in New York City. Life was much simpler but not necessarily better.

While his father "Joe" worked long hours in the penny arcade, his mother Annie was a stay-at-home mother, as most mothers of that generation. After Bill's two sisters, Pearl and Nesbith arrived, Annie was busier than ever as it was before we had refrigerators, washing machines, dryers, and other modern conveniences.

When talking pictures and all the musicals arrived during the Depression, it brightened everyone's lives. When Bill's mother Annie went to the movies for the admission of price of fifteen cents, she also received glass dishes. Today, "Depression glass" is considered an antique. Saturday afternoons were special for the young Bill. His mother gave him eleven cents, ten cents for admission to the movies and a penny for candy. He loved watching all the cowboy movies, the Tarzan series, and newsreels in black and white.

The highlight of this childhood was spending summers at his grandparents' farm in Burlington, Vermont. His father Joseph would put him on the train with a tag around his neck with his name, his destination, and his grandparents' name and address. His father gave the conductor a fifty-cent tip and, since Bill had to change trains, an additional fifty cent tip to give to the Rutland railroad conductor that would bring Bill into Burlington. His Uncle Archik Perelman would meet the train in a horse-drawn carriage and bring them to Zayde Issac "Itsik" and Bubbe Sarah Rivkah Perelman's home outside of town.

Bill Cohen

For a youngster living in the city, staying on a farm was very exciting. For breakfast, his grandmother punched two holes in a fresh egg, and Bill would slurp it up. He would also have warm milk that his grandmother had just milked from the cows that morning. As he got older, Bill learned how to milk the cows and pile the hay. He also enjoyed going places with his grandfather in the horse and buggy.

Growing up, Bill did not have many toys, so he improvised and created his own. He read many books from the public library. When Bill was six years old, he started Public School 167. He also attended Hebrew school. When he was thirteen, he observed his *bar mitzvah,* the ceremony marking his entrance into Jewish adulthood, not as the special boy on the *bima,* the raised platform in the front of the synagogue but as part of a large group of boys his age. Bill remembered that the rabbi's son had most of the readings and most of the spotlight during the service. Afterward, everyone noshed on sponge cake and wine and then returned home. Many years later, Bill would make up for his own underwhelming rite of passage by throwing a large bar mitzvah celebration for our son Jay, complete with Friday night and Saturday services and sit-down-dinner at a lovely restaurant in Plattsburgh, New York.

Around this time, Bill started helping his father on weekends in the penny arcade business. Times were not the best, and Bill was able to supplement the family income. One day, a member of Tammany Hall came to the penny arcade and had Bill arrested for "gambling." Bill landed up in jail for a few hours until his father got him out.

After Bill graduated from Boys High School, he planned to live with his widowed grandmother Bubbe Sarah and attend the University of Vermont. That was not to be. When his grandmother came to New York City to attend his graduation, she passed away of a heart attack. Dreams of UVM ended.

Bill worked three summers as a bellhop in the Catskill Mountains in Sha-wan-ga [Also known as Shawanga] Lodge. He saved enough money to attend Pace Institute evening classes to study merchandising. He also worked at the World's Fair in 1938 and 1939.

Since Bill was interested in business, his uncle Archik suggested he apply for a job working up north in the small Pearl's Department Store chain. He started his Pearl's career managing a store in Malone, New York. While there, he met my brother Eli and my cousin Elliot Helfand, who also worked for Pearl's. One day, Bill was visiting Elliot at his parents' home in Brushton, New York. He saw a picture on Rose and Ruby's piano of a beautiful woman with dark wavy hair and high cheek bones. Bill asked Elliot the woman's identity. "That's my cousin and Eli's sister Fradel," Elliot told him. "She lives in Coney Island with my Aunt Ethel and Uncle Joe."

"I am going to marry that woman," Bill said.

Soon after, the three men decided to come to New York City for a long weekend. My brother and cousin both had dates, and, on Bill's insistence, arranged a blind date for Bill with Frances Cohen. The rest is history.

My Romances

Since today is Valentine's Day, I thought I'd write about my romances until I met my true love. The saying goes, "You have to kiss many frogs until you meet your true love." Well, I knew many frogs.

I was a senior in high school when I experienced my first romance. I thought that Bernie had the bluest eyes and the curliest hair. I was completely infatuated. The economy wasn't the best. So, our date consisted mostly of walking and holding hands. Bernie was my date for the Senior Prom. Although he wore a very shabby suit and I borrowed a gown, I thought I was lucky to have a date to the prom with the guy I adored. Things changed after I graduated high school. I got my first job in a toy store for $10 a week six days a week. Bernie didn't have a job, so in the fall when the leaves died, so did our romance.

That New Year's Eve was not a happy one for me. Instead of giving me a gift on Christmas Eve, my boss told me he did not need my services anymore. Worse yet, I did not have a date!

Time passed. Both my girlfriends were going steady. Their problem was that their boyfriends did not have a car. Charley, one of their friends, did, so my girlfriends urged me to date him. I was not especially fond of him, but we all were fond of his car. Conveniently, Charley was able to drive the three couples around. The six of us even went to the midnight show at the Apollo Theater.

Fran, "Charley" and Millie

Financially, things improved for me when I finally got a good bookkeeping job that I loved. When summer arrived, I was given a week's vacation with pay. I decided to spend it in a hotel in the Catskill Mountains. The hotel had all the ingredients for romance, including swimming, boating, entertainment, and dancing. The first night at the hotel, I was seated next to a tall, handsome guy named Harry. We spent the whole week enjoying all the activities, and by the end of the week, I was completely infatuated with him. We continued dating after I got back from my vacation. I was having a great time as I was dating Charley on Saturday and Harry on Sundays. That situation ended a month later when Charley wanted to get engaged. How could I marry Charley when I was wild about Harry?

When Harry invited me to a formal dinner dance at the Astor Hotel that his firm was sponsoring, I was delighted. I purchased a new black taffeta gown with a matching purse and matching shoes. When Harry arrived to take me to the dinner dance, looking handsome in a tuxedo with a corsage in hand, I was ecstatic. But shortly after the dance, he stopped calling. I was really hurt. I guess I was wild about Harry, but Harry wasn't wild about me.

I didn't date anyone interesting for quite a while. Now that I was almost twenty-two years old, my mother was eager to see me settled with a handsome, rich, Jewish man. Cupid stepped in to help. My brother Eli, our cousin Elliot, and their friend Bill Cohen were all working for my Uncle Paul, who had a chain of department stores in Upstate New York. The three of them came home one weekend to visit each of their families. Bill, who had seen my picture at my Aunt Rose and Uncle Ruby's house, asked Elliot and Eli to fix me up on a "blind" date.

31

That night I finally met my true love. Bill and I were attracted to each other immediately, and there was instant chemistry from the first moment we saw each other that was to last for a lifetime. My mother's prayers were answered—almost! Bill was handsome and Jewish. Rich he wasn't, but two out of three was not bad!

It was to be a long-distance romance. Bill made the eight-hour trip to see me as often as he could, but we only saw one another less than ten times before we married. We wrote every day—I still have his letters in a blue satin bag I keep in my dresser! We had so much in common: our love of reading, our respect for education, our desire for children, and our large, close-knit families. We soon realized that our family trees even had connecting branches as both our families came from small villages near to each other in Lithuania.

Even more astounding, we had actually "met" over twenty years earlier as children through those connections. In 1919, when I was two years old, I contracted the Spanish flu. When my lungs filled up with fluid, the doctor saved my life by cutting an incision into my back to drain them. It was recommended that I spend time away from our tiny apartment in Brooklyn and breathe country air. My mother Ethel quickly made arrangements for the two of us to visit her stepmother's sister Ittel [Levinson] and her husband Archik Perelman, who lived on a farm in Burlington, Vermont. While there, Ethel and I were visited by Archik's brother and sister-in-law, Itsik and Sarah Perelman; their daughter Annie [Perelman] Cohen, and her six-year-old son, Bill. There is an expression "My father married my mother. Why do I have to marry a stranger?" Well, Bill didn't feel like a stranger to me.

On Valentine's Day, 1940, Bill made a special trip in to see me. We went to the movies and then went out for sundaes at an ice cream parlor. After spending three hours watching *Gone with the Wind*, Bill must have thought I was Scarlett O'Hara, and so he asked me to marry him. I must have thought he was Rhett Butler, because I said yes. We were married that summer and have spent the last sixty-six years celebrating Valentine's Days, our anniversary, and our love for each other.

Marriage—1940 Style

On May 1940, Bill and I officially became engaged when Bill presented me with an Elgin wristwatch. We began planning our wedding. My brother Eli and his fiancé Zelda had planned a big Sunday afternoon wedding for August 18. To make it convenient for our out-of-town guests to attend both weddings, we planned a smaller event for two days later on Tuesday evening, August 20, 1940.

We had a difficult time writing the wedding invitation as both my maiden surname and Bill's surname were Cohen. To make it even more complicated, thanks to the officials at Ellis Island, both my father's and future father's-in-law names were Joseph Cohen. Even our mothers' names matched: My mother was Ethel Annie Cohen; Bill's mother was Annie Ethel Cohen. To make it clearer, we used the first letter of our first names as the middle initials of their names, left our mothers' first names completely off, and had the invitation printed as shown here.

Our wedding was not elegant. However, Bill and I made a handsome couple under the *chuppa* (wedding canopy), me in my rented wedding gown and floor length veil ($8), Bill in his rented tuxedo ($7), and both of us so happy we glowed. (Priceless!)

After the religious ceremony, the guests were served tea sandwiches, fruit, and wedding cake. Unfortunately, by the time

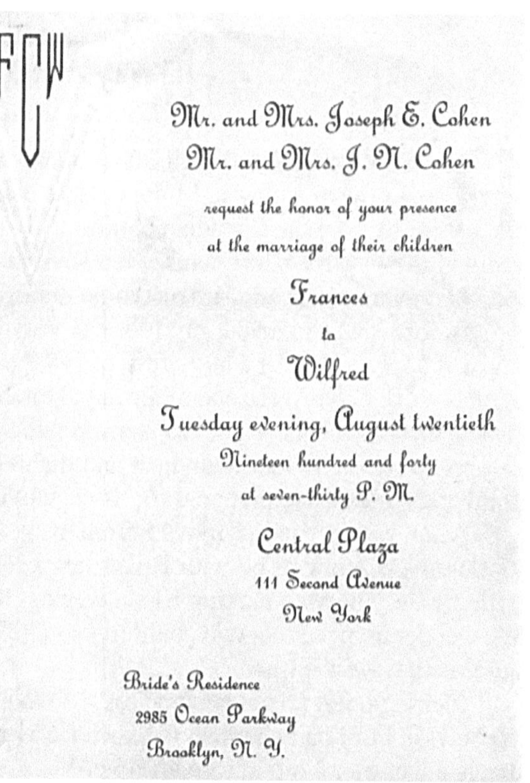

Mr. and Mrs. Joseph E. Cohen
Mr. and Mrs. J. N. Cohen

request the honor of your presence

at the marriage of their children

Frances

to

Wilfred

Tuesday evening, August twentieth
Nineteen hundred and forty
at seven-thirty P. M.

Central Plaza
111 Second Avenue
New York

Bride's Residence
2985 Ocean Parkway
Brooklyn, N. Y.

the photographer finished taking our wedding pictures, most of the guests had left and most of the food was gone. We did keep the bride and groom figure from the top of our cake, which we still have in our china cabinet today.

Bill and I had a two-day honeymoon at the Hotel New York in a bridal suite at $10 a night. On Thursday morning, my cousin Elliot and my Aunt Rose met us at the hotel in his car to drive us to Malone in upstate New York where we were to make our first home. As this was before the Thruway and the Northway, the trip was over ten hours long. Bill and I planned to take advantage of long trip on the road by cuddling contentedly in the back seat, but that was not to be. The back seat was filled with suitcases, wedding gifts, and home furnishings, including a huge table lamp. Aunt Rose was prone to carsickness and needed to sit next to the window in the front seat. And so, we started the first chapter of our life together as Mr. and Mrs. Wilfred Cohen with me in the front seat between Elliot and Aunt Rose and with poor Bill squeezed into the back seat, balancing the lamp on his lap for the entire trip.

Newlyweds

By September 1940, Bill and I spent our first few weeks as happy newlyweds living in Malone, New York, a small village only a few miles from the Canadian border. Bill had been working there for two years in the North Country and loved it. Since it was a new way of life for me, there were many adjustments to be made.

Before I was married, my life was very different. I worked in a job I loved, a bookkeeper for a large firm called the Dixie Dress Shop in the heart of New York City. At the end of the day, I took the subway home to Brighton Beach for five cents. I arrived home to the apartment I shared with my parents, warmed by the steam heat and the delicious aroma of my mother's homemade meals she prepared for us each evening.

After we married, I moved from New York City to a tiny town in Upstate New York to be with Bill. I left a job making $19 a week to live with a man who was making $18 a week. That was before Women's Lib. We were convinced that two could live as cheaply as one. We quickly found out that that wasn't true.

Please do not misunderstand me. I loved being a married stay-at-home housewife, but I had so much to learn. I was now expected to prepare three meals a day on an old kerosene stove. My mother and mother-in-law were not much help living 350 miles away. Besides, they never cooked from a recipe, as their measurements consisted of a *bisl* (little) of this and *shtik* (piece) of that. My mother-in-law sent me more detailed recipe books and a mix master, and Aunt Rose, who lived close by, also gave me lessons. I eventually learned to cook and bake, but not without much trial and error.

My first experience cooking rice was a disaster. I started out following the directions exactly, using one cup of rice to two cups of water. After ten minutes, I checked the pot, and it didn't look like one cup of rice would be enough for my husband's hearty appetite. So, I added more rice and then more water and then more rice and then more water. By the time Bill came home for dinner, there were three huge pots of cooked rice sitting on the stove. For the next two weeks, we lived on tomato rice soup for lunch, rice casseroles for dinner, and rice pudding for dessert.

Soon after we were married, Bill was transferred to a Pearl's department store in Rouses Point, New York. We were now farther from our family, and I often felt lonely. In the winter, the temperatures were always at least thirty degrees lower than New York City. The natives always described the winter weather as "a February thaw is thirty below and a hell of a blow."

As the months wore on, I found it very difficult to adjust to all the snow and cold. Besides, our three-room furnished apartment was not fully winterized. The big potbelly stove with its dirty ashes sat in our living room, and that room was always too hot. The kitchen was just right, but the bedroom was always only forty degrees. I felt like Goldilocks!

I missed all the good things that the Big Apple had to offer. I missed browsing and shopping in the big department stores. I missed eating in Italian and Chinese and Jewish restaurants and in the automats. I missed the theater, the big glamorous movies houses with vaudeville shows, and Radio City Music Hall and the Rockettes.

But with a loving husband who was an optimist, I gradually changed my attitude. I started to look at the beautiful scenery of the Adirondacks and Lake Champlain and all the advantages a small town had to offer.

Our Saddest Thanksgiving

As newlyweds, Bill and I spent our first few weeks living happily in Malone, New York. As we were surrounded by many relatives, including my Aunt Rose and Uncle Ruby and my cousin Elliot, and many of Bill's friends, it made it easier for me to adjust to leaving New York City and relocating to a small town in the North Country.

Therefore, we were very unhappy when Bill was transferred to work in the Rouses Point store, where the only people we knew were the store manager, Jack and his wife Margie. We had no sooner made the move and settled into our new apartment when we received two invitations. The first was a formal invitation to my best friend Millie's wedding, which was to take place in New York City at the beginning of November. The second was a verbal invitation from Bill's boss to celebrate Thanksgiving with his wife and eight other guests at their beautiful home.

I was so happy for Millie to hear of her upcoming marriage. Life had not been easy for her. Her father was killed in an accident when she was only eight years old, and her mother struggled to raise Millie and her two brothers. Her mother had repeatedly said to Millie, "Life is like a deck of cards, and sometimes you get a raw deal." I hoped Millie's marriage to her wonderful boyfriend would change her luck.

As Bill had just started work in Rouses Point, he could not get the time off, so I went down to New York City by myself for a few days. I had a wonderful time attending the wedding and staying with my parents, whom I had missed very much. As soon as I arrived home, I wrote a letter to Millie saying how much I enjoyed the wedding and how much I hoped she would be as happy as Bill and I were.

Three weeks later, on the Sunday before Thanksgiving, I received a phone call from Millie. I was devastated to learn that her husband had taken violently ill on their wedding night as a result of a bleeding ulcer and had died three days later. Through her tears, she said that she would be alone for Thanksgiving weekend. Could she please come up north to stay with us? I quickly agreed and made arrangements to meet her at

Fran and friend Millie

the railroad station the Wednesday night before Thanksgiving. I told her of our plans to have dinner at Bill's boss's home and assured her that, under the circumstances, Margie would welcome Millie with open arms.

On Monday, I visited Margie and told her the sad story of Millie and her tragic loss. I was shocked, therefore, when Margie told me that, even though she felt very sorry for Millie, my grieving friend could not come to the Thanksgiving dinner party. Margie explained that her dining room table was only big enough to accommodate twelve people, and her china and silver set were only sets of twelve as well. Having an extra guest would upset her carefully planned dinner arrangements. "Besides," Margie stated, "it would be unlucky to have thirteen people!" However, Margie made it clear that she still expected Bill and me to attend despite the fact that we had a guest waiting at home. As Jack was Bill's boss, we had no recourse but to go to their home for dinner and leave Millie behind.

I spent two sleepless nights dreading the idea of telling Millie that she would be spending Thanksgiving dinner alone. When Bill and I picked her up late Wednesday night, I broke the news to her. I explained to her that we would prefer to stay home with her, but we could not antagonize Bill's boss by not showing up for Margie's dinner party.

On Thanksgiving Day, I went to the party with a heavy heart. I felt so guilty as Millie had traveled all the way from New York City to receive comfort from her oldest, dearest friend, and I had let her down. It was the saddest and most unforgettable Thanksgiving I ever had.

Millie and I spent Friday through Sunday morning together. I made a belated Thanksgiving dinner at my apartment and comforted her as best I could. On Sunday morning, again with a heavy heart, I put her on the train for her return trip to New York City.

Five years later, Millie remarried. She and her husband had two beautiful children, and she had a happy life. It took a long time, but finally Millie had been dealt a winning deck of cards.

Our First Child Is Born

Bill and I lived a short time in Rouses Point, New York before he was transferred to a Pearl's in Alburgh, Vermont. We were close to Burlington and, more importantly, close to family, including many of our aunts and uncles who lived in the area.

We were overjoyed to learn we were expecting a baby. In order to be closer to the Burlington hospital, I stayed with my mother's youngest sister, my Aunt Ruth and her husband, Isadore Kropsky. I was due in March, four months after the United States entered World War II. A few days before her due date, the doctor had discovered that I had come down with toxemia. He had hoped that I would not deliver the baby for a few days as it was not good for the baby or me. We were so thankful that after a long delivery, Laura Beverly Cohen was born healthy, and I was fine.

The first time I lay eyes on my daughter, she did not look like the beautiful babies I remembered from pictures and advertisements. The doctors had had to use forceps, so Laura's face was slightly bruised and misshapen. The first thing I said was, "How will I marry her off?" The nurse said, "Isn't she too young to be married?" In a few days, once the effect of the forceps wore off, she was a lovely baby.

Despite that initial "un-forecep-unate" reaction, I can't express the happiness we experienced as Bill and I held our newborn. We knew our life would never be the same, as everything would revolve around her.

After ten days, Laura and I were released from the hospital. (Today mothers go home in two days and are much better.) I don't like to admit that I was a very nervous mother when I first brought Laura home. I followed Dr. Spock to the letter. Instead of holding and cuddling her more like I should, I let her cry. I always think every couple should have their second first. Laura would have been a happier baby!

I was very frightened when I realized that from now on that this bundle of joy was my responsibility. I wasn't an experienced mother. But I learned to manage although it was more difficult in 1942 than today. Today we have sterilized formulas and Pampers. I had to sterilize baby bottles. I had to wash the diapers in an old-fashioned wringer washing machine and hang them up to dry on a clothesline no matter what the weather. But Bill and I were thrilled. We were a family!

Laura Beverly Cohen

Our Life in St. Johnsbury, Vermont

A few days after I arrived home from the hospital in Burlington with our newborn, Bill told me we would be moving again in six months. The United States had entered World War II on December 7, 1941, after the bombing of Pearl Harbor. Many of the people who worked in the Pearl's department stores spread through Vermont and New York were being drafted to face combat in Europe and the Far East. Fortunately, as we had a new baby, Bill was exempt from the draft. Uncle Paul, ever the businessman, decided that it would be wise to close some of the stores until the war ended. Paul told Bill that he was being reassigned to manage the St.

Johnsbury, Vermont, store for ten months until the lease on the store was up.

Bill and I were initially very unhappy about the move. We had already moved twice since we were married, and we knew that we would only be in St. Johnsbury for ten months. We did not look forward to finding new doctors, learning where best to shop for clothes and food, and, most importantly, making new friends. Having a new baby was a full-time job, and I would still have to find time to pack up the house and unpack once we were moved. We would miss the little house we were renting and the big extended family that had been our support for the past two years.

Fran holding Laura

Our disappointment was countered by our gratitude that Bill was not drafted as were so many men of his age—including many of our relatives and friends. Bill had a job, we had a beautiful baby girl, and we had each other.

By the beginning of May, Bill left to start his new job. As soon as he found a suitable apartment, he came home to help me pack. Within the month, we were settled into our new home with our three-month-old daughter.

Since we were going to be there for a few months, we never even fully unpacked the boxes. We were fortunate to make friends with some other young couples after we arrived who readily helped us to adjust to the new community. As for Bill, he was happy finally to be a manager of a store. He still had a great deal to learn, as the following story illustrates.

Soon after Bill took over the St. Johnsbury Pearl's, an attractive middle-aged woman came into shop late on a Saturday afternoon. She left the store with a new dress in a shopping bag, and Bill closed that night with a sale and a smile on his face. Bill's happiness ended when she walked into the store Monday morning with the dress in the same bag. Mrs. Saturday Shopper told Bill she showed the dress to her husband, and he didn't like the way it looked on her. She requested a refund and left, saying she hoped to return later in the week to pick out another dress.

As promised, Mrs. Saturday Shopper came in late Saturday afternoon and purchased a new dress with unfortunately the same results: a discontented husband, a refund, followed by another late Saturday afternoon shopping trip. On the third Sunday, Bill was purchasing a newspaper at a store across the street from one of the town's churches. He saw Mrs. Saturday Shopper arm in arm with her husband entering the church wearing the most recent exchange. On Monday morning, she returned to the store, again requesting a refund. My Bill, always the diplomat, sweetly said, "That's funny! I saw you on Sunday morning going into the church with your husband, and you looked absolutely lovely in it!" The woman glared at Bill, grabbed the bag, and left the store. Bill never saw her again. Bill later heard through the grapevine that Mrs. Saturday Shopper pulled that stunt on every new store manager in town.

In February 1943, the lease on the St. Johnsbury store ended. We were eager to move on as Bill had just been offered a job with a store in New London at twice his Pearl's Department Store salary. We once more packed up and moved to Connecticut.

The War Years in New London, Connecticut

In 1943, Bill, Laura, and I moved to New London, Connecticut, as Bill had obtained a job in a retail store that included his working in advertising, a field that he loved.

By the time of our move, the United States was fully involved in the war that was raging across the globe. Service men and women were deployed to Europe and Africa to fight Hitler and the Axis countries; others were shipped to Southeast Asia to battle Japan. Those families who had relatives serving in the armed forces were especially affected. Everyone did a lot of praying for our military to win the war and come home soon.

President Franklin Roosevelt was very eager to bring the war to a close as soon as possible while, at the same time, to bring the country out of the deep Great Depression that had hit the country beginning in 1929. He changed our peace-time economy to one fully engaged in wartime. Our factories were converted from places making cars to tanks, boats to battleships, clothing to uniforms, and desired goods to needed ammunition.

On the home-front, life also changed drastically during the war years. Many items we took for granted, including sugar and coffee, were now rationed. Many were forced to give up their cars. While the men serviced overseas, women who were not in uniform were working in factories. Judy Garland and Vivian Leigh were replaced with a new role model, Rosie the Riveter. Everyone was encouraged to buy war bonds, and Golda Meir made trips to the United States to meet with President Roosevelt to plead the case that the country accept Jewish refugees who were trying to escape the Nazi concentration camps. No one complained, as everyone accepted these changes as part of the nation's patriotic duty.

Americans also felt very fortunate in that the United States and Canada were one of the few countries who escaped the direct impact of the war. Cities in Europe, including London, were bombed daily, and many of its residents were sleeping in shelters. We weren't even aware of the atrocities that were being committed against millions of people in the "work camps" throughout Europe established by Hitler and his henchmen.

Personally, I was very fortunate as I had my husband home. Initially, Bill was not drafted as those with young children were exempt. As the war dragged on and more and more people were called up, Bill found out that the back injury he had sustained in his teens while playing semi-pro football was serious enough to classify him as 4F.

New London was a military hub. Laura's first memories were watching the soldiers in their uniforms passing by the house in trucks on their way to the naval submarine station in Groton, Connecticut.

Apartments were few and far between. Fortunately, Bill and I found a lovely apartment on a bus route, which was ideal as, like many others, we had given up our car. The bus took Bill to work and took me and Laura to stores and, in the summer, to a lovely beach on the ocean. Bill worked full-time days in the store and worked four nights a week in an ammunition factory.

Meanwhile, as new parents, Bill and I realized that children did not grow up like lettuce. We had a few incidents that terrified us. The first one was when Laura fell to the floor from our bed and held her breath for a very long time. Another incident was even more frightening. We lived on a very busy street with lots of traffic, and one day I was walking home, holding Laura's hand. When she saw her father across the street, she pulled herself out from my grip and walked right into the road. The driver of the car stopped right in front of her, got out of the car, and almost fainted from fright. To be honest, I almost fainted as well. After the two incidents, we treasured our little girl more than ever.

Looking back to that time, I always have felt a little guilty. While the war years had an impact on our lives, the effect certainly paled in comparison to the difficulties of many of our relatives and friends. We were grateful when the war in Europe began to wind down in 1944, and the war in Southeast Asia ended in August 1945. Bill and I were eager to have another child. Bill wanted a boy. My father wanted a grandson as "anyone could have a girl!"

Due to some health problems, I had been told that I might not be able to conceive again. We were delighted, therefore, to learn just as the war was

ending that I was pregnant. Our son was born nine months later. To this day, I can remember the pain of delivering him and his huge shoulders. But he was beautiful and healthy, and we now had a rich man's family: a girl and a boy. We named him Jay Ira. His Hebrew name was *Yosef Itzhak ben Shalom*, Yosef after Bill's father Joseph who had passed away of lung cancer the year before and *Itzhak* after Bill's grandfather's Itsik.

Jay Ira Cohen

Potsdam

The war was over, and Bill was concerned that his job in New London, Connecticut, was insecure as the owner of the store's son was returning from overseas. When my brother Eli Cowen offered him an opportunity in 1948 to become a partner in his retail-clothing store in Potsdam, New York, we decided to make the move.

Unfortunately, there was a big housing shortage after the war. We were packed up and ready to move in with Eli, who had been divorced from his first wife Zelda. The night before we left, Eli called to say he had just remarried, and we couldn't stay with him and his new bride Rosalind (Roz).

Our first winter in Potsdam was not easy. The only place we could find to live was a new house in the middle of a large field with no trees. The kitchen was so small that I could stand in one place, open the fridge, and take a chicken out, turn around and wash the chicken in the sink, turn again and place the chicken in the oven. The rest of the house contained a small living room, two tiny bedrooms, and a cramped bathroom. As it was situated on top of a windy hill with no trees, the house was hot in the summer and cold in the winter. In addition, the basement always had water, the depth depending on the amount of rain we had gotten.

In addition to the cramped quarters, we had other big adjustments. Laura, our six-year-old daughter, started first grade, and she came home with everything but an education. First, she came down with measles. One month later, she came down with the chicken pox. Each time she got sick, she gave the illness to Jay, her two-year-old brother.

Spring finally came and my parents were finally able to visit us. The couch in the living room opened to a bed, so our living room became our guest room. We bought a double collapsible bridge table and our living room also served as a dining room. Laura wanted to take piano lessons, so my parents bought her a small reconditioned upright piano that just fit on one wall.

Things were running smoothly. Our children and we made friends. The empty field across the street from the house became a site for traveling carnivals and circuses, which we enjoyed.

We especially loved going to the outdoor movie theater in the summer. The admission for a whole family was nine dollars. We would dress the children in pajamas, and they slept on pillows in the back of our red station wagon while we watched the movie.

And sometimes our children unexpectedly provided the entertainment. One day, Laura, who was around seven years old, discovered an old pile of letters in my dresser. She decided to play post office and deliver them to our neighbor's mailboxes. The only problem was that the letters she had found were the love letters Bill and I had exchanged during our engagement. I only found this out when a neighbor called to ask why a passionate letter from a lovelorn man was in her mailbox.

When Jay was around five years old, he heard Bill, who was a volunteer fireman, talk about the beautiful new fire truck in town. Jay and a friend thought it would be great to get a first-hand look. After Bill was at work, Jay's friend dialed the number, and Jay reported a fire at 55 Waverly Street. Meanwhile, Bill, who was a member of the volunteer fire department, heard about the alarm, ran out of the store, got into his car, and sped home. When the new truck pulled up in front of the house, the fire chief yelled to Jay and his friend, who were standing in the driveway. "Where is the fire?" They sheepishly pointed to the chimney across the street that was spewing smoke from its coal furnace. The fire chief threatened Bill with a fine. Bill and I were not into spanking our children, but I am sure Jay never pulled that stunt again.

Things changed when I realized that I was pregnant with my third child. Babies are little but take up a lot of room. Where would I put a highchair in that small kitchen? And where could I squeeze in a crib and a playpen?

Bill and I, however, always planned on more children. Marilyn Renee Cohen was born on Labor Day 1950. How fitting! As my doctor had a 12 noon golf date, I accommodated his

Bill, Laura, Jay, &
Fran pregnant with Marilyn

schedule by delivering our second daughter a little after 9 a.m., allowing him plenty of time to get to the links.

Picture our home with a baby. In addition to our couch, two chairs, and an orange slightly off-key second-hand piano, the living room was filled with a playpen, a baby carriage, toys, and—as we did not have a foyer or a garage—shoes and boots all over the floor. The "master" bedroom now had a crib and a dressing table for the baby. The kitchen, with the addition of the highchair, was even more crowded. When Laura and Jay's friends came to our house each to walk together to school, they had to hold their lunch boxes and school bags over their heads in order for the next child to squeeze into the room.

Despite the crowded and less than ideal conditions, we were happy in our little home. We called it our "Rubber House," as it stretched whenever it was needed. The tiny living room was often filled with friends, food and drink, and music provided by a talented neighbor who was able to work magic on the cracked keys on our piano.

We were even happier when my brother Eli and his wife Roz announced that they were going to have their first baby. Two months before the baby arrived, I planned a baby shower for her. The day of the shower, we collapsed the playpen and opened the double bridge table. Bill took our three children to my brother's. I served tea sandwiches, dessert, and coffee to eight women. We all enjoyed opening the baby gifts.

Soon after that, I could no longer put off the gall bladder surgery that I needed since my first symptoms appeared when I was pregnant with Marilyn. The surgery was difficult, and the recovery even more so, especially with three children, including a toddler who never let go of my skirt. It was fortunate, then, that Bill and Eli waited until I recuperated fully to tell me that the store could not support two growing families. Yes, we were moving again!

In a short time, with Uncle Paul Pearl's direction, it was decided that Bill would open a store in Keeseville, New York. Bill rented a room in the small town one hour south of the Canadian border and spent the summer overseeing the conversion of an empty building to another of the Pearl's chain of stores. I stayed in Potsdam to sell the house.

One day the agent called to tell me that he was bringing a couple to see the house. The sun was out, and it was 90 degrees outdoors and indoors. But miracles do happen. By the time they arrived, the sun went down, and a strong wind came up. The basement happened to be fairly dry that week. When the couple arrived, they said our place was the coolest in town and our basement had the least amount of water. The house was sold!

Our family was ready to start a new chapter in our lives in Keeseville.

Keeseville

Once we had sold the house in Potsdam, Bill went by himself to find a house for us in Keeseville while I stayed home with the three children.

Not many houses were for sale that summer, but Bill finally called at the end of June to tell us the good news. He had found a large four-bedroom colonial just a block from the store. He told us to start packing as we would be moving at the beginning of August, a few weeks before school started. The house needed a "few" repairs that he hoped would be completed before we moved in. Just before he hung up, he said, "Oh, by the way, don't give the cat away. Fluffy is coming with us to Keeseville!"

Bill initially stayed in a rented room over the summer while managing the now-open Pearl's Department Store. He came home at the end of August to help us pack. Although we had hoped to be settled in our new home well before Labor Day, the closing on the house was delayed. The first day we were able to move in was September 1, two days before Marilyn's second birthday and five days before school started. As a result, Bill had not been able to arrange for the "minor" repairs he said the house needed.

The day of the move, a Saturday, a team of men filled up a Pearl's Department Store truck with all of our furniture and possessions and arranged to meet us in Keeseville. After traveling three and a half hours in our red station wagon, Bill, Laura, Jay, Marilyn, the cat, and I finally arrived. As we pulled into the driveway, I got my first glimpse of our new home.

The outside of the house was beautiful. The house was situated on a pretty lot with lots of bushes and flowers. The house itself was a Victorian colonial, white with green shutters. A screened-in porch was on one side of the front of the house; another porch ran along the right side; a third porch ran along the back of the house on the left. The previous owners had planted beautiful gardens along the front of the house and in the back.

We walked across the lawn and climbed up five wooden stairs onto a small porch that lead to the front door. We entered the house through a small, enclosed foyer that led into a very large living room and dining room with lots of windows that spanned the entire front of the house. A beautiful oak archway separated the two rooms.

But when I entered the kitchen, I couldn't believe my eyes. The room was a disaster! In the center of the room was a big old fashioned non-working black stove. Above the stove was one light bulb hanging from a wire from the ceiling. Outside of that lone light bulb and the outlet that would run the refrigerator we had brought from Potsdam, there appeared to be very little working electricity in the entire kitchen. The unfinished wood floor was covered with torn linoleum. The old metal sink had only one faucet. When I turned the water on, there was no pressure, just drips of cold, rusty water because the house was connected to an almost empty well. In place of kitchen cabinets was a filthy, dark pantry. It was obvious that lots of mice had moved in before we did. I then knew why Bill told me to bring Fluffy. Our house was cat heaven!

My eyes filled with tears. Bill saw how unhappy I was and tried to comfort me. "I'm sorry I could not find a better house, but please be patient. Nothing can happen over the Labor Day weekend," he said. "But on Tuesday, I have arranged for the carpenters to tear down the pantry. I promise you that you will have a kitchen you will be happy with."

The children and I went to explore the rest of the house. Behind the kitchen was an unheated shed. Upstairs, the four bedrooms had lots of windows, which only served to shed light on how shabby the rooms actually were. Like the kitchen, the floors were unfinished and covered with chipped linoleum. All the rooms were in desperate need of a fresh coat of paint and new wallpaper. Laura and Jay were the first to notice that there was no bathroom upstairs, only the small dark bathroom next to the kitchen.

The basement was dark and damp, with several small rooms, including one with a large coal furnace and another with a wringer washer. In these days before electric dryers, I knew I would have to carry baskets of wet clothing upstairs through the kitchen and hang them on the clothesline that was strung up in the back of the house.

The furniture from the tiny house in Potsdam barely filled the rooms. To add to our problems, Laura's beloved second-hand piano that we brought from Potsdam had fallen off the moving truck. It had survived, but barely, and it was even more off key than it was in Potsdam.

By Sunday night, everyone was tired, exhausted, and upset. Laura and Jay had not wanted to move in the first place as it meant a new school and new friends. After living her first two years in a tiny box, Marilyn was terrified of the big, dark house. She clung to my skirts for dear life even more than she had in Potsdam. The only one who was happy was Fluffy the cat, who had already polished off several of the mice in the pantry.

The next day was Labor Day as well as Marilyn's second birthday. Bill had the day off as all the stores were closed. Always the optimist, he declared that *all* of us—except Fluffy—deserved a holiday. To cheer the children up, we took them to the store, which was closed for the holiday, and let Laura and Jay select clothes for the first day of school. Marilyn, the birthday girl, got a new dress.

Since our electric stove wasn't connected, we all had lunch of hot dogs and French fries in the small diner near our house. Now that we finally had a dining room, we decided to celebrate Marilyn's birthday in it. We even decorated the room, so it didn't look so shabby. Thanks to Bill's shopping the day before, we had a store-bought birthday cake and ice cream on pretty paper plates. Little did we realize that Marilyn's second birthday would be the first of many happy occasions we would celebrate in that room for the next thirty years.

The next morning, Bill left for the store. He could not help me any more with the move as it was the day before school opened—one of the biggest shopping days of the year. I put Marilyn in the stroller and walked Laura and Jay across the keystone bridge that spanned the Ausable River and then up the hill to the school to register them for classes that Wednesday.

When we arrived back at the house, a crew of men from the town were digging up the sidewalk in front of the house so they could connect us to town water. When we entered the house, the carpenters were tearing down the pantry. Brightening, I realized that without the pantry, I was going to have a nice big kitchen with two windows, quite a contrast from the tiny kitchen we had lived with in Potsdam. I was very encouraged until the electrician came to connect our new electric stove. He told me the stove was fine, but the wiring in the rest of the kitchen was so faulty that if we did not take care of it immediately it could cause a fire and burn down the whole house. We needed to hire an electrician quickly.

Later that afternoon, there was knock on our door. Mary Cross, a neighbor who lived a few houses away, introduced herself. She told me that she had been in Pearl's earlier in the day and Bill told her I needed help. She said she would be glad to lend a hand. Mary and I started a warm relationship that day that continued for many, many years. She helped us make our house into a home.

We began to meet the neighbors. Across the street lived the Halens, who raised chickens. When the wind blew the right way, we could smell them. And we were treated—literally—to the sight of chickens running around with their heads cut off. Alice, our neighbor to the left, housed a beauty salon in the front rooms of her home. In the front yard was a huge evergreen that we would learn would be festooned with Christmas lights every December. Ironically, Frenchie, the neighbor on the right, also had a beauty salon on the first floor her home. It looked like I would never have to worry about having to travel far to get my hair done! Frenchie also had a huge, green lawn that would be a wonderful place for our children to play when they met her children. As the months went by, the kitchen and the rest of the house underwent the needed repairs. We replaced the kitchen cabinets, rewired the whole house, and redid the plumbing. We replaced the flooring and bought new furniture for the living room. We began to enjoy our life in the big house on Five Vine Street.

Flag Day

My parents, who had escaped religious persecution in Eastern Europe, continually told me from the time I was a little girl what a wonderful country the United States was and how lucky we were that we lived here. When both of them had arrived in America, years before they had met, they both had been so eager to be Americanized that they had changed their names to less foreign sounding names. My father changed his name from Yossel to Joseph, and my mother changed her name from Ettel to Ethel. In addition, although they were working long hours in factories during the day, they both had attended night school to learn how to speak and write English. They were very proud to be citizens of this fine country.

As a result, I have always felt very emotional when I stand up to pledge allegiance to the flag or when I hear a patriotic song, especially Irving Berlin's "God Bless America." Many years ago, however, my patriotic enthusiasm resulted in one of my most embarrassing moments.

We had moved to Keeseville in 1952, and Bill managed Pearl's Department Store on Front Street. As he was very civic minded, Bill joined the local chapter of the Kiwanis. In early spring of 1955, the Kiwanis' planned a special meeting that would be open to all the wives of the members. Plans included a potluck dinner, and I was asked to bring a potato salad. At the time, I was six months pregnant with my fourth child, and I was excited to have the opportunity to have a night out to meet more people in our community and to wear the new maternity dress I had bought for the occasion. It was an unusually warm early spring day, and I spent the day making the potato salad, shortening the new dress, and taking care of my other three children. By the time Bill and I left for the meeting, I was tired and thirsty.

When we arrived at the hall fifteen minutes early, I was pleased to see that a fresh bowl of punch was waiting for the guests when we arrived. I poured myself a cup of the delicious red beverage and then went back for seconds and thirds. At six o'clock, the president of the Kiwanis asked everyone to stand up to pledge allegiance to the flag. I stood up, put my hand over my heart, and—Crash!—promptly fell to the floor in a dead faint!

I vaguely remember being carried into another room. When I regained conscious, I was lying on a couch, and the local doctor, a member of the Kiwanis who was fortunately at the meeting, was standing over me. "Young lady," said Dr. Temple sternly, "you should not be drinking so much alcohol, especially in your delicate condition!" It was only then that I found out that the punch was laced with rum. Talk about making a great impression on my new neighbors! I learned a valuable lesson that day: Never drink punch without first making sure that it isn't spiked!

The Unforgettable Halloween

BY 1958, Bill and I were settled with our four children in our home in Keeseville.

Bill was very civic minded and president of the town's Chamber of Commerce. That spring, he received a letter from a young optometrist who had just completed his time in the military. Dr. Jerome Resnick was interested in opening a practice in upstate New York and wanted to know what Keeseville had to offer.

Bill immediately wrote back a glowing letter about our small town. He stated that people in surrounding communities liked to shop in Keeseville as it was a thriving community with many retail stores and a large factory that manufactured television cabinets. Many doctors had practices in Keeseville, but there were no other eye doctors. Bill also said that Dr. Resnick would love living in Keeseville's location. It was on beautiful Lake Champlain with its opportunities for boating, fishing, and swimming. There were three golf courses nearby, and if the doctor liked to ski, Lake Placid and Whiteface Mountain were less than an hour away. "Most importantly," Bill stated, "half the population of Keeseville wore glasses and the other half needed them." Bill ended the letter with an invitation for Dr. Resnick to visit

Keeseville and stay as a guest of the chamber in a local hotel so the young doctor could learn more about the community.

Two weeks later, Dr. Resnick arrived, and as promised, Bill and other members of the chamber showed him around. The young doctor was impressed and asked if office space was available. Only one store on the main street of town was available to be converted into an office, but Bill gave him the name of a reasonable contractor. By the end of the summer, with Bill commandeering the construction, the office was completed, and Dr. Resnick was settled in an apartment and was ready for his new patients.

By this time, "Jerry" was a friend of the family. During one of his visits to our house, Jerry confided in us that his parents, who were from the New York City area, were very unhappy about his move to what they considered a small hick town in upstate New York. Jerry was encouraging them to come for a visit and see for themselves that he was happy, business was good, and the people in Keeseville, especially the Cohens, were wonderful, friendly, refined people.

Fall came, and with it came an invitation for Bill and me to attend a Halloween costume party at friends' house the Saturday before October 31. Since parking was difficult at the hosts' house, Bill and I arranged for neighbors to pick us up at 6:45 p.m.

Everyone, including Bill and I, invited to the party really enjoyed putting together the outfits for the costume party. The night of the party, the two of us were upstairs in our bedroom getting into our costumes. I had chosen to dress as Sadie Thompson, a "lady of the night," who was a main character in a popular movie of the day. I was garbed in a very tight, low-cut sweater and a very short skirt. My hair was heavily teased, and I wore tons of eye make-up and lots of cheap jewelry. Bill was dressed as a hobo complete with size 52 pants tied with a rope, a ratty shirt covered with patches, a wig with a huge bald spot surrounded by lots of orange hair, and a clown nose that honked. An empty rum bottle finished the look.

At quarter of seven, our children called up to tell us that someone was at the door. Thinking it was our neighbors, we decided to make a grand entrance. I sashayed down the

stairs, swinging my hips and twirling my pocketbook to beat the band. Bill stumbled behind me, taking swigs of his "rum" and honking his nose.

When we got to the bottom of the stairs, we were mortified to realize that the "someone at the door" was not our neighbors but Jerry and his parents, who stared with utter horror at the "wonderful, friendly, and refined" Cohens!

After a long moment of stunned silence, Jerry introduced us to his folks, and we hastily explained our appearance. Our neighbors, also costumed, soon arrived, and we were whisked off to the party, but not before we invited the Resnicks to dinner the next day to meet the real Cohens.

Jerry's parents must have been somewhat appeased. Jerry kept his office for another 30 years until his retirement. When he married, he and his wife Lil remained our friends. But every Halloween, Bill and I remember our unforgettable Halloween almost fifty years ago.

My Love Affair with an Old Oak Table

For over fifty years, I've had a love affair with my old oak dining room table. Everyone prizes something more in his or her home than others do, and for me it is a 100-year-old piece of furniture.

Our family had recently moved to Keeseville from a tiny house in Potsdam, New York that had little furniture. One day, a customer shopping in our store told us that their parents were giving up their home on the farm and were moving in with them. They asked if we knew anyone who would be interested in buying their parents' old oak table and chairs.

Bill and I told them that we would love to look at the dining room set. We fell in love with it the minute we saw it. The table was over fifty years old, but it was in good shape, had beautiful lion claws at the end of the legs, and would fit perfectly into the dining room of our old Victorian house. It could seat six, but when the four oak extension leaves were added, there was even more to love! We paid ten dollars for the table and five dollars for each of the six chairs. As soon as the table arrived in our home, it became part of the family.

If the table could talk, it would talk all about the wonderful times it shared with the Cohen family. Birthdays, anniversaries, Thanksgiving, Passover—all were celebrated around the oak table.

The table would also say that it felt elegant when it was dressed up in a beautiful damask tablecloth and matching napkins, and when the food was served on Bavarian china with sparking silverware and the drinks were served in stem glassware.

Even at more casual times, the table was always laden with tons of food. When anyone asks me if I was a good cook, I always said, "I'm not a gourmet cook. I just cook quantity!" With four growing children, a hungry husband, and lots of company, I had no choice. And the oak table always supported my spreads.

The table was not only for dining. The children preferred doing their homework on the table instead of the desks in their rooms. Sundays through Thursday nights during the school year, the table was buried in schoolbooks and papers. The table was also used as a game table. The children played card games like Fish, War, and Old Maid and board games like Monopoly and Scrabble. They put together 1000-piece jigsaw puzzles and set up toy soldiers in formation on its surface. On rainy days, a double sheet draped over the top turned the table into a tent, a stagecoach, or a playhouse. Bill and I played bridge and card games with couples. Several times

Another generation around the old oak table!

a year, Bill served as host for his poker game. The dining room was filled with smoke as the men drank soda and beer and snacked on Brach bridge mix and peanuts.

Our four children still talk about the birthday parties they celebrated with friends around the oak table. The menu was always the same: hot dogs and rolls, Heinz vegetarian beans, and potato chips for the meal, followed by a homemade birthday cake. The birthday child always got to help bake the cake from scratch or as the years went by, from a mix. Then the child helped frost the cake with confectionary sugar frosting and decorate it with the candies that came on a cardboard sheet that spelled out Happy Birthday and held the candles.

The table had its problems. One day there was a huge crash in the dining room. The old chandelier that hung above the table fell into the middle of the table. We were thankful that no one was hurt and that the table escaped with just a couple more scratches. Within a couple of days, the chandelier was replaced, and the table was back in service.

Time passed, and the table became the gathering place for celebrations of high school and college graduations and engagement parties. The children moved away, and we began spending more time in our cottage on Lake Champlain. In 1982, with retirement looming, we decided to sell the house in Keeseville and split our time between the cottage and Florida. We sold most of our furniture, but the oak table moved with us to the cottage. It fit beautifully in the large dining area. In the summer of 1983, we celebrated our retirement with a party of over fifty people. We set out tables and chairs on the lawn, but everyone came into the cottage for the buffet that was set up on our precious oak table.

Time passed, and grandchildren came to spend time at the cottage. The oak table again became the play table, as they loved to paint, color, and play games on the table.

By the year 2000, Bill and I were in our eighties, and we realized it was getting too much for us to maintain the cottage and decided to spend all our time in Florida. We were delighted when our son Jay and daughter-in-law Leslie opted to buy the cottage and keep it in the family. We could not make it up to the cottage for two summers. When we moved into Coburg Village in 2006, however, we finally had the opportunity to go up to the camp. When we visited, we realized that another generation is now enjoying the table. The top is a bit more worn and scratched, but the lion paws still shine and look like new. And so, our family's romance with the one-hundred-year-old table continues.

Family Pets

As with many parents, Bill and I tried to be "super parents." Since Bill and I never completed college, one of our greatest priorities was that our children should have the advantage of a college education. When our children were infants, we fed them a spoonful of pablum and said, "You *are* going to college; you *are* going to college!" As they grew older, we surrounded them with books, music lessons, and sports opportunities. We also wanted them to have a sense of responsibility, so we had pets— many pets. In many instances, we had more problems with the pets than with the children.

Our first cat was named Fluffy. We brought her with us from Potsdam when we moved into our very old-fashioned house in Keeseville. One of the problems with our house was that lots and lots of mice moved in before we did. Fluffy turned out to be a good cat. The children loved her and Fluffy solved our mice problem. Of course, she was not perfect: We were very unhappy when she used the arms of our new sofa as a scratching post.

One morning when I was in the basement putting laundry in the in dryer, the phone rang in the kitchen. I rushed upstairs to answer it. When I came down after the phone call, I finished loading the dryer, closed the door, and turned it on. I immediately heard a terrible thumping noise. I immediately opened up the dryer door, and Fluffy jumped out. I was very shaken but was happy that the cat had used one of her nine lives and was just fine. A short time later, Fluffy was in a car accident, and we had to put her to sleep. Since the children were devastated, we promised them a new cat.

Fortunately, our neighbor's Siamese cat had a litter of beautiful kittens, and our girls selected not one but two to bring home. Romeo and Juliet were trouble from the beginning. I called them the two prima donnas. They were fussy eaters and cried constantly. At that time, we had an old-fashioned bathtub with claw legs. To put in a shower, we had to box in the bottom of the bathtub and leave an opening for repairs. When winter came and with it the cold weather, our two prima donnas refused to go outside to relieve themselves. Unfortunately, they also would not condescend to use the litter box in the basement and preferred crawling into the opening of the bathtub. Once our noses discovered their secret, we had no choice but to give Romeo and Juliet away. They turned out to be the most expensive animals as we had to replace the old-fashioned bathroom years before we planned to do so.

When our daughter Marilyn was leaving for college, we knew that our youngest daughter Bobbie would be lonesome. We acquire a big Irish setter that we named Moose. Moose was beautiful, lovable, but not very bright. He loved to take long walks, an opportunity that was limited by our busy schedules.

One morning, I became very ambitious and decided to make a big batch of blintzes as we were having company. Blintzes are a Jewish dish that is similar to French crepes, but they are even more time consuming as each pancake is filled with

Marilyn, Bobbie and Moose

a cheese, sugar, and egg mixture and then fried. I was so proud of myself when I completed the preparation of three dozen blintzes. I had lined them up on clean white towels on the kitchen counter, ready for the next step in the recipe. Just as I was about to start frying them, I was called away. When I returned a half an hour later, Moose had pulled the towels down, all the blintzes were on the floor, and the dog was having the feast of his life. I was ready to kill him, but by that time, he was family.

Bobbie, of course, grew up and left for college. We kept Moose for a few more years but found it difficult to take care of him as we were still working. We finally decided to give Moose to a family with children who lived on a farm. We missed Moose, but we knew he had room to run and children to take care of him in his new home.

Looking back, we realized that we must have done something right as parents as all of our children and grandchildren used their college education to have successful careers and make us proud. As far as our pets, we did not do the best job of raising them. We were far too lenient and let them train us. Perhaps we would have done better if we had a Dr. Spock manual as we had for our children!

Fiftieth Wedding Anniversary

*I*n celebration of their fiftieth anniversary, the four children and their spouses made a party for them in our home. Mom wrote the poem below to commemorate the occasion and read it aloud.

Here is the handsome guy I married,
Here is the pretty gal who promised to obey.
After loving one another for fifty years,
What is there to say?

My hair has turned to silver,
Bill's teeth are on the dresser in a tray.
I've lost that girlish figure,
And Bill can't hear what I have to say.

Now that we are retired, love Florida
and the cottage on the lake,
Let us celebrate our fiftieth anniversary
with ice cream and cake.

In addition to the party, we all chipped in to give Mom and Dad a Caribbean cruise, the first of their lives. Mom wrote us the following note after the party:

CLOUD 9

Dear Children,

Please notice the address above. We still haven't come down from Cloud 9.

The party was a huge success and one of the highlights of our lives. We still can't believe that all you children are sending us on a "Cruise." It's a dream come true. So—Thank you. Thank you. Thank you. After being married 50 years, Dad and I feel that we accomplished the most important thing in life—we have wonderful children and precious grandchildren.

Love,
Mom and Dad

Please Be Patient with Us

Now that we are senior citizens, we reminisce about the happy times all our family spent during the summer at our cottage on the New York side of Lake Champlain.

When we purchased the cottage, Bill and I were younger and had a lot of energy, so we enjoyed doing all the things we loved to do, including swimming, boating, gardening, and entertaining all our family and friends.

Time went by and all the children married and presented us with eight precious grandchildren. Everyone loved spending time at the cottage.

But thirty years passed, and Bill and I slowed down. So, at the end of the summer of 1997, I wrote this letter to my children:

September 30, 1997

Dear Children,

Thanks for planting flowers in front of the cottage and putting down wood chips so we do not have to weed. Also thanks for helping us out all summer.

Dear children, we have aged, and there is a great generation gap. We have many problems all senior citizens have, so please be patient with us.

When you visited us this past Labor Day, Dad and I were sitting in the family room watching television. Marilyn, you rushed in wearing you jogging clothes and said, "Dad, it's so hot in here!" You opened all the windows. I replied, "Marilyn, we have not been jogging so we were cold. So please be patient with us."

An hour later, Bobbie walked into the family room and said, "Dad, the television is so loud! How can you stand it?" I replied, "Bobbie, your father is not wearing the hearing aid as it is being repaired. So please be patient with us!"

Laura, we all appreciate it when you do some of the cooking as I tire easily. But please do not be insulted if we don't always eat the delicious gourmet dishes you make as they are too spicy for our sensitive stomachs. Also, we cannot eat the vegetables you cook *al dente* as we cannot chew them.

But most of all, be patient with us when your father and I repeat the same story three times as we don't remember that we told them before.

Thirty-five years ago, your father got impatient when his mother kept repeating the same stories. I'd kick him under the table and tell him to be patient. So, history repeats itself. Be patient with us, and I hope someday in the future your children will be patient with you.

Having you visit us makes our summer complete.

Lots of love,
Mom and Dad

Five years after I wrote this letter, we were delighted that our son and daughter-in-law bought the cottage, and it is still in the family. Now our great grandchildren enjoy visiting.

College

Bill and I always regretted that we did not have a college degree, but times were different in the 1930s during the Great Depression.

When I graduated high school, there was no way that I could afford to go to college. I got a job right after graduation as a bookkeeper. Most of my salary went to pay the rent of my parent's apartment. Bill's grandparents had planned to help Bill with college tuition, and he hoped to move to Burlington to attend University of Vermont. Those dreams ended when his widowed grandmother died after attending his high school graduation, and she left no provisions to pay for his education. Since he did not have the advantage of a college degree, he went into the retail business and spent many years associated with Pearl's, a family-owned department store chain that sold lower end merchandise. Things changed in the late sixties when the Northway and the big box department stores open. We found it difficult to compete. Fortunately, we had the opportunity to open the Village Bazaar, a very nice ladies' store that catered to the career women. It was successful, and we decided to close Pearl's and concentrate on the Bazaar.

While our children were growing up, we kept telling them, "You are going to college! You are going to college!" Beginning in 1964, our dreams of making sure our four children had college educations became a reality. Our daughter Laura graduated from Geneseo with a degree in special

education, a new field that was opening up. Soon, our other children followed our oldest daughter's footsteps. Our son Jay graduated Union College in 1968, Marilyn graduated from SUNY Albany in 1972, and our youngest Bobbie graduated from Plattsburgh State in 1978. Two of the children completed master's degrees. All of our grandchildren have also received their undergraduate degrees and even completed advanced degrees.

At times, however, their education almost backfired on us. When Laura came home for Thanksgiving her first year, she began swearing up a storm, using four letter words that had never come into my home before. I decided to turn the tables on her and started using them myself. When Laura expressed surprise that I was swearing, I responded, "I'm paying $2000 a year to send you to college so that you can come home and swear like a sailor. I figured I could do it for free!" Laura never swore in my presence again.

Jay also got a lesson in humility after he finished his first year at Union College in Schenectady, New York. He had taken an Introduction to Business course, and, like many college freshmen, Jay thought he knew everything. Jay commented, "Mom, how have you been able to help Dad in the business without a college education? For example, how do you know how much money you need to purchase merchandise for the coming season?" I told him, "I look up last year's figures, make the necessary adjustments based on inventory, and plan accordingly."

Not backing down, Jay asked, "So how do you know where to shop and what to buy?" I told him about Irwin Magerfield Associates, a buying service with whom we contracted to help us with choosing the clothes. In addition, I told him we had lived in Keeseville for sixteen years, and we had a sense of what women liked and wore.

"So how do you know what sizes to buy and how much of each?" Jay asked.

"We generally sell more size 14s and 16s, so I shop accordingly," I said. I also told him much of the clothing business was common sense. "I learned this all from the seat of my pants, Jay," I said firmly "And if we hadn't run the business successfully, we couldn't have afforded to send you to a good college like Union. So, I guess I know quite a bit without having a fancy college degree!" Jay never brought up our lack of a college education again.

Bill and I take pride in our children and grandchildren's education, but we also take pride in the fact that we were self-taught, sometimes the best kind of education a person can have!

Heading to Florida

October 1982 was a very exciting time for us, and a turning point in our lives. After forty-five years of being involved in retail, Bill and I were selling the Village Bazaar. We were finally retiring.

The road to retirement actually began a year earlier. Our cousins, who lived in Southern Florida, had invited us to visit them for ten days. In order to get to our plane, which was leaving from Montreal, we had to drive in a snowstorm. Just after we crossed the border into Canada, our car hit an icy patch, and we skidded into a snowbank. Thankfully, there was no damage to the car, and we were able to make our flight.

When we got to Florida, we got our bags and drove our rental car to our cousins' condo. They greeted us at the pool. It was 85 degrees and sunny, quite a contrast from the blizzard conditions and 15-degree temperatures we had left in Keeseville. The first thing I said was "This is paradise!" Right then and there, Bill and I decided that we would spend the next winter in Florida as retired people. When we got back up north, we put the building up for sale.

Florida's sunshine was not the only motivation to our retirement. Business in the Village Bazaar had slowed down. When the Northway was completed, we lost many of our customers to the attraction of the new malls in Plattsburg, only 15 miles north of Keeseville. It was hard to compete!

In addition, in October 1981, we had sold our big house in Keeseville and had been commuting from our cottage. The curvy roads were difficult in the summer and sometimes downright dangerous in the winter. We also were not looking forward to spending another winter in the cottage, which was not fully insulated and was very desolate December through March. I cannot express how happy we were when the building that housed the Village Bazaar finally sold.

We had a going out of business sale in the fall of 1982. By Thanksgiving, we had arranged to rent a condominium near Fort Lauderdale for three months starting January 1, 1983. We were officially snowbirds.

Our First Home in Florida

I cannot express how exciting it was spending our first winter in Florida. After enduring so many long winters in small towns in Upstate New York and Vermont, it was a welcome and delightful change to be in the Florida sunshine and not have to deal with snow and ice. We spent many hours at the condo pool, swimming and socializing with the neighbors. We went out to eat frequently, and we enjoyed relaxing, shopping at the many stores in the area, and just spending time together.

Bill and I discovered that we had many first, second, and third cousins living in Florida whom we had not seen for many years. We enjoyed visiting each other, often going out to lunch. Bill and I especially enjoyed going to one of the many Jewish style delicatessens as we did not have them up north where we lived.

Saturday night was always special. By four o'clock, the pool had cleared out as everyone went back to their apartments to change for dinner. We were usually seated in our restaurant of choice by 4:30. Most of the restaurants featured "Early Bird Specials," which offered full dinners from soup to dessert. The food was delicious and, as long as you ordered before 5:45, the prices were ridiculously low. And we even had enough for leftovers the next day!

After dinner, we usually went back to the condo's social hall for live entertainment. Every Saturday, the condo provided singers, dancers, magic acts, concerts, and comedians. Some of the performers were a little long in tooth and a little past their prime. No matter! They sang songs we knew, danced to music we had danced to ourselves in the Thirties and Forties, and told jokes that made us laugh. We looked past the bleached hair and the wrinkles and loved every minute of the performance.

The second year we went to Florida as snowbirds, we rented an apartment in Margate, which was located between Boca Raton and Miami. As much as we loved the complex in which we rented, we loved visiting our cousins who lived in nearby Hawaiian Gardens. Not only was their condo conveniently located, but it also had very beautiful grounds with lots of flowers, shrubbery, and even ponds with bridges over them. As we wanted to spend even more time in the warm weather, we realized that it was more sensible to buy our own condo than to continue renting. We purchased a fully furnished condo in excellent condition in Hawaiian Gardens with an extra room for company.

When we returned north that spring, we told our close friends from up north, Harold and Lil Shubert, about our time in Florida. They asked us if we could find a condo in the same complex for them to rent, and they were so pleased they returned for several years. In addition, we were very close to our son-in-law Larry's parents Doris and Ernie Shapiro, who lived in Saratoga Springs. One winter, they came to visit us and loved Hawaiian Gardens so much that they bought a condo in a building right near us. We spent many good times over the next several years with our relatives and close friends, most who were snowbirds like us.

Looking back, we retired at the right time. We no longer had the responsibility of being in business, but we were still young, still healthy, and still had lots of energy. It was so much fun shopping and walking in the malls, going to shows and movies. We loved driving to the ocean and walking in the sand. Bill often played golf.

By 1986, all four of the children were married, and our children blessed us with many grandchildren. In the summer, the family gathered at our cottage on Lake Champlain. And now, in the winter, our children and grandchildren came to visit us in our beautiful condominium to swim in our swimming pool, to eat out every night at the many nearby restaurants, and to go to the ocean to sit on the beach and bounce in the waves. Life was good.

In 1983, the musical *La Cage Aux Folles* opened on Broadway with its show stopping, "The Best of Times Are Now." For Bill and me, this was truly the best of times.

Changes: Our Second Home in Florida

The year 2000 brought many changes in our lives. After spending many years as snowbirds, we both had aged and did not have the energy to maintain two homes any longer. More importantly, two events occurred that made us realize that it was time to sell the cottage, move out of Hawaiian Gardens, and move into a different living situation.

People change and so do neighborhoods. The first major event was having our car stolen. One morning, instead of finding our Toyota in the usual parking space, we found an empty spot and lots of broken glass. When the police arrived, they informed us that there had been a rash of car thefts that was being done by a group of teenagers. The police returned our car that very afternoon, but it was in very bad condition. We had to trade the car in for a new one.

Six months later, on Christmas Eve, a second incident occurred that was more frightening. As we were getting out of our car after going to the movies, two very large men attacked us in the parking lot of Hawaiian Gardens. The first man demanded that Bill give him his wallet. Bill, furious, refused, so they sprayed Bill in the face with mace. Luckily, Bill was wearing glasses, so his eyes were not affected by the attack. The second man demanded that I hand over my purse. When I told him that I did not have one with me, he pulled my wristwatch off my hand. Bill started shouting, "Help!" As neighbors came out of their apartments to investigate, the two men fled. We were so lucky that we weren't hurt or killed. We decided that night that it was time for us to move into a gated community where it would be safer.

Upon recommendations of friends, we decided to move into Wynmoor, a large, gated community about one half hour from Hawaiian Gardens. The condo had more security as well as a number of other amenities, including a nurses' station, bus services for shopping, a restaurant on the premises, and a large auditorium that held over 500 people that provided movies and live entertainment.

In order to afford the move into Wynmoor, however, we had to sell both the condo in Hawaiian Gardens and our cottage up north. After a very long summer with no bites on the cottage, our son Jay and his wife Leslie decided to buy the cottage from us. We were delighted as the cottage was still in the family and we could still visit. Soon after that, we sold the condo in Hawaiian Gardens, packed up our belongings, and moved to our new place in Coconut Creek.

Unfortunately, during the time of the move, Bill had not felt well and complained of stomach problems. Only six days after we moved into our new condo on Bermuda Circle, Bill collapsed and was rushed to the hospital. He was diagnosed with colon cancer and was scheduled for surgery. I called our daughter Marilyn from the hospital, and she flew down the next day to be with me. No more than twenty-four hours later, I admitted to Marilyn that I was having chest pains. By Tuesday, Bill was in one hospital room on the fifth floor, and I was across the hall. Although Bill got through the surgery in good shape and I was diagnosed with just a mild heart attack, it was not a good start to our new life.

Over the next five years, Bill and I enjoyed Wynmoor despite Bill's declining health. We were able to take advantage of the amenities and made many friends. Our children, however, were becoming more and more concerned about our living so far from them and encouraged us every time they visited to consider moving back up north to be closer to them. Both of us were not ready to give up our independence. We dug in our heels and stayed put.

We Return to Upstate New York

This all changed in 2005, when Hurricane Wilma ripped through Southern Florida. After spending a frightening day inside the condo as the storm raged outside, we were able to go outside and assess the damage. Our building had only minor damage, but many others in Wynmoor had extensive damage, including torn-off roofs, fallen wires, and hundreds of trees on their properties that had been downed by the Category Four Hurricane. For three days, the electricity was out. We didn't have air conditioning, the food in our refrigerator was going bad, and we couldn't even boil water on the dead stove. The elevators were not working. When we finally were able to drive our car to the supermarket, all the traffic lights were out, making extremely dangerous to navigate the streets. In the middle of all this, I fell while getting out of our car after a trip to the grocery, and I broke my femur bone. That was the final straw. We did not want to live through another hurricane, and I no longer could do what I had done before my accident and the rehabilitation that followed. Our children insisted that we move back north so they could be there for us, and this time, we said yes.

We were so lucky that Marilyn and our son-in-law Larry located an available apartment in Coburg Village, an independent living facility only four miles from their home. While the two of them made all the arrangements for us to move into a one bedroom, two-bath apartment, the rest of the children pitched in to help with the move. Laura, our oldest daughter, flew down from Philadelphia and helped us pack. Our son Jay

Coburg Village, Rexford, New York

flew down a couple of days later. On April 25, 2006, the two of them drove us to the airport and went back to Wynmoor to supervise the movers and finish last minute packing and cleaning. Once the realtor arrived for the final check, Laura and Jay started their two-day trip up north in our car.

Meanwhile, we had flown into Boston, where our youngest daughter Bobbie picked us up from the airport. After a two-day stay in her home, she drove us to Coburg. When we got to our new apartment, Marilyn and Larry had already arranged to have a new couch delivered. The moving van arrived a couple of days later. Laura dropped Jay off at his home in Pennsylvania and continued onto Coburg to help us move in. By May 1, we were settled in our new apartment, close to our children, and away from hurricanes.

Two and a half years after moving into Coburg Village, I had to make the biggest adjustment of all. Bill passed away on November 20, 2008. I made the decision to stay in Coburg Village as it was now my home. After a few months, I made the decision to downsize into a smaller apartment, where I am able to keep busy with my many friends and the many activities at Coburg Village.

The Weather

The weather plays an important part of our life. At times, we wish that we could change the weather, but as we have learned it is one of the things in life we cannot change.

Sometimes prayers help. On two occasions, our prayers were answered when we planned outdoor receptions. One was for the retirement party Bill and I planned at our cottage on Lake Champlain during the summer of 1983. The second was at the wedding reception for my granddaughter that was held on my daughter and son-in-law's front lawn in Clifton Park in October 2007. At both parties, the weather was perfect: sunny, 72 degrees, with no wind. We considered it a miracle!

Our prayers did not work when Bill, my daughter Marilyn and I had to travel from Keeseville to Rockland County for our son Jay and our future daughter-in-law Leslie's engagement party in December 1970. A Nor'easter started the day we were supposed to leave, so we delayed the trip until the next morning in hopes the weather would improve. Unfortunately, the snow only got heavier. By the time we arrived in Albany, the New York Thruway was closed. Determined not to miss the party, we decided to take Route Nine for the rest of the trip. The roads and visibility were terrible. At one point, Bill stopped at a railroad crossing as the gate was down and the lights were

Marilyn after a snowstorm, Keeseville, NY 1953

flashing. The snow was so thick that Marilyn, who was sitting in the back seat, thought we were actually on the tracks and began screaming in fear. When we all calmed down, we continued on the trip. We arrived in Pearl River at 11 o'clock at night, sixteen hours after leaving Keeseville for what should have been a four-to-five-hour trip. It was one of the most difficult trips we ever made.

In 1980, the year before we retired, our cousins invited us to visit them in Florida. When the day of our flight arrived, we left our cottage on Lake Champlain to drive to Montreal, the closest airport. When we crossed the border to Montreal, the snow was piled so deep that drifts were at places two stories high. As we crossed over a bridge near the airport, Bill lost control of the car, and we did a complete 360-degree turn, landing in a soft snowbank. Fortunately, there was no damage, so we were able to continue the trip to the airport. When we arrived in Florida, it was 85 degrees, and our cousins welcomed us in summer attire. Bill and I looked at each other and said, "This is paradise!" We couldn't change the weather, but we could change our location. Right then and there, we decided that before next winter, we would sell our business, have a going-out-of-business sale, and spend our winters in Florida and summer at our cottage by the lake.

We were fortunate to be snowbirds for many years. It was the best of both worlds: Beautiful summers on Lake Champlain and warm, balmy winters in Florida. We thought we had it made—until Hurricane Wilma hit in 2005.

At that point, Bill and I were living full time in a condominium in Wynmoor, an over-fifty housing complex in Coconut Creek, Florida. The Weather Channel and local officials had warned us in advance of the incoming hurricane, and we had made sure to purchase water, canned food, and extra batteries. The night the hurricane hit, we did a lot of praying. The winds and rain were very strong, and we were very frightened. We were so thankful that our building had been spared any serious damage. We woke up to no electricity and no air conditioning in the 85-degree heat. For the first few days, we stayed in our condominium, living on the canned goods that we had purchased before the hurricane. When the electricity finally came back in our condominium, we decided to go food shopping for milk, eggs, and other food to restock our pantry and refrigerator. At that point, we were able to see the actual extent of the damage in the area. We saw lots of fallen trees, some of which had crashed into parked cars. With all the wires down and traffic lights out, getting to even the supermarket was almost impossible.

When we finally got to Publix, the store was dark and eerie as it was powered by back-up generators. We learned as the week went on that thousands of trees had been destroyed in our residential area. More tragically, a number of other residential areas, including Hawaiian Gardens, the original complex we had moved out of only four years before, were so badly damaged that they were unlivable and eventually had to be completely torn down.

In the middle of all this stress, when I was getting in the car to take another trip to the supermarket a week after the hurricane hit, I caught my foot on the curb while trying to get out of our parked car and broke a bone in my leg. That was the final straw. Our children felt strongly that we needed to get out of Florida and its hurricanes and move back up north. By spring,

2006, we were settled in Coburg Village, four miles from my daughter and son-in-law. At Coburg, we don't need to drive, as the shuttle takes us everywhere. Our children are close enough so they can go shopping for us if the weather is too bad. So, when bad weather comes, we are able to just look out the window and enjoy our cozy apartment. Now we can be thankful for the snow so that grandchildren can ski, the rain that makes our flowers and gardens grown, and the beautiful sun that makes us all happy.

Sympathy Card for a Toyota

*I*n 2006, my mother and father moved from their condo in Florida to Coburg Village, an independent living facility only four miles from my husband Larry and me. Our father especially resisted the move in part because one of the conditions was that they were to give up their car, Dad's beloved Toyota Camry. After our parents were delivered safely to the Fort Lauderdale airport to fly to their new home, my siblings finished packing up the apartment and then began the 1300-mile trip back to Saratoga County.

Soon after they were on the road, Laura and Jay realized that the glove compartment in the car didn't have the registration. It was still in Dad's wallet. They were a little nervous about being stopped, but fortunately that didn't happen. They also realized that the back windows in the car, which had never been opened the entire time my parents owned the vehicle, were sealed shut from the Florida heat. They were not able to get them opened on their trip.

Once the car was unpacked, Laura drove the car to our curb in front of our house, where it sat until our daughter Julie picked it up in August. After her visit, she "caravanned" with Larry and Adam, who had his Honda

Civic, on the drive back out to Julie's job in Colorado and Adam's first year at Stanford Law School in California. Julie and Adam played with the back windows for hundreds of miles with no luck at lowering them. Someplace in Kansas, however, the rubber on the windows finally gave up. The windows went down easily. Julie drove that car for another 80,000 miles before the engine died. Here is the note my mother wrote to Julie when that happened:

Dear Julie,

So sorry to hear the sad news that your Toyota died. The good news is that you had it for almost four years.

Grandpa loved the car and took very good care of it. He also brought the car to the car wash often, so it always looked good. The Toyota had a good life. It spent winters in Florida and summers in the Adirondack Mountains overlooking Lake Champlain. It was a lucky car as it wasn't recalled as many of its relatives were.

Grandpa hated to give up the car when the family felt he was not up to driving it anymore, so we gave it to you.

Julie, you enjoyed the Toyota in all kinds of weather. You drove it to work 50 miles each way, and you and Sam enjoyed taking the car on vacation. We gave the car to you with love. Sorry it didn't last longer.

Love,

Grandma Fran

Wedding Ring Blues

On August 20, 2008, Bill and I celebrated our sixty-eighth wedding anniversary. We are truly blessed with a large family who brings us lots of pleasure and are there for us when we need them.

After our long marriage, I am walking around with a cane, a walker, and a husband, but no wedding ring on my left hand, even though I have had three wedding rings in my life.

Let's start back in 1940 when Bill and I got engaged. Bill could not afford to get me an engagement ring. Wristwatches were in style during the Great Depression, so instead, he bought me a beautiful gold Elgin wristwatch. The watch stopped working after a few years and was replaced with others. When we were married, Bill bought me a plain gold wedding band. I wore Wedding Band Number One for fifteen years.

When our youngest daughter arrived in 1955, we bought a new automatic washing machine and a new electric dryer. What a pleasure! No more schlepping wet laundry upstairs to hang on a clothesline!

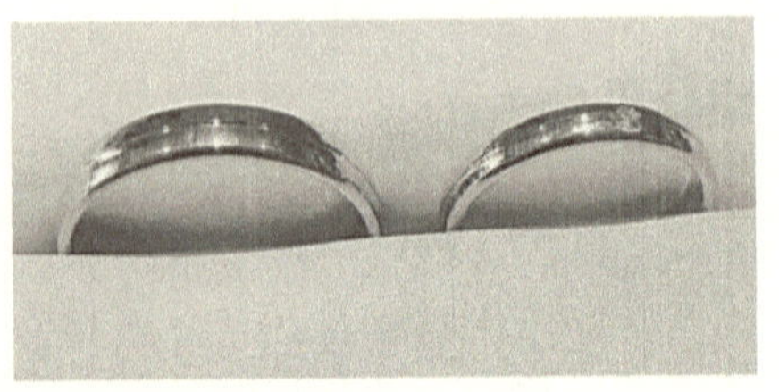

One day after washing diapers, I discovered that I had no wedding ring on my finger. Some washing machines eat socks. I guess my machine prefers wedding rings.

A month after I lost my ring, Bill had to have minor surgery that required a short hospital stay. Bill drove us up to Plattsburgh. Instead of going directly to the hospital, however, my husband of 15 years drove directly to Lippa's jewelry store. "I am not going to be in a hospital bed and have you walking around with four children and no wedding band," he told me. So, I now was on Wedding Band Number Two.

In 1965, my mother Ethel passed away. My father Joseph said it would please him very much if I would wear the diamond engagement ring that he bought for my mother in 1912 for the princely sum of $100. For our thirty-fifth anniversary in 1975, Bill and I decided to have a new setting made for my mother's diamond engagement ring with a matching diamond studded wedding band. Hence, Wedding Band Number Three!

Since I was a child, I always dealt with a problem with psoriasis. In the past year, the skin condition appeared on my left hand on my wedding finger. As a result, I asked my daughter to place both the engagement ring and the wedding ring in her safe deposit box for safekeeping. The fingers on my left hand are finally beginning to clear up, and I'm looking forward to wearing my rings again.

Until then, I may not have a wedding ring on my finger, but I have my husband with me, and that is better than any ring I could own!

The Cottage

September 17, 2009 was a very bittersweet day for me. That was the day the Cohen family cottage on beautiful Lake Champlain was demolished. Personally, it was a difficult day for me to realize the cottage where we had spent forty summers was temporally a pile of logs. The cottage is gone, but all the wonderful memories will linger on. The good news is that it is going to be replaced with a beautiful new, modern home.

Let's start from the beginning. Many of our relatives had what we called camps on lakes in Northern New York and Vermont, and we enjoyed visiting them. We hoped that one day we would have one of our own.

In July 1966 we were told that a person we knew had a camp for sale in a small town on Lake Champlain only 30 minutes from Keeseville. That

evening Bill and I went to see it. The camp was very rustic, just a large building made of logs that consisted of one big room. Two parts were sectioned off with thin wall boards for the two bedrooms. The wallboards did not reach the ceiling, so there was no privacy. A large bar with benches that could accommodate at least ten people separated the kitchen from the dining and living areas. The small bathroom was the only room that was completely enclosed. Bill asked me what I thought. I looked out on the lake. Just then the sun was setting. The view was magnificent. I said, "Buy it!" Bill was so surprised, as I was the one who always said, "I'll think it over." By August 1966, we were proud owners of a camp on Lake Champlain.

A few weeks later we received the following letter from friends in Scranton, Pennsylvania. It made us smile:

Dear Fran and Bill,

Good luck on buying a camp. But we are worried about you, Fran. With a large family and working full time, we hope it won't be too much for you. Is it a boys' camp or a girls' camp?

Love,
Rose and Harry

I guess Rose was right. I looked up the word "camp" in the dictionary, which defined a "camp" as a temporary place for children out of the city. From then on, we tried to remember to call it our "cottage" when speaking to our downstate friends and relatives.

Although the "camp" needed lots of repairs and wasn't my dream home, it was one of the smartest moves that Bill and I ever made. The property was reasonable, and we could afford it.

As our family grew, so did the camp. In 1968, thanks to the financial help of our daughter Laura and her then husband Richie, we built on a large family room with huge windows facing the lake. Over the years we entertained lots of company and hosted lots of parties. All our children and our eight grandchildren enjoyed the camp for many, many years.

When Bill and I reached our eighties, we found it was too difficult to keep up the cottage and put it up for sale. We were so happy when our son Jay and his wife Leslie offered to buy it as it would still be in the family.

Ten years have passed. Jay and Leslie are now grandparents. Jay recently retired, and Leslie will join him soon. They plan on spending much more time at the lake. So, they are replacing the old "camp" with a beautiful new cottage. They are so excited and can't wait until it is built. The structure may be new, but the sunset will be the same. May they enjoy many happy years in their new home on the lake.

Jay & Mom at the new cottage 2009

Cohen's Villa

Mom wrote the following in 1973. When Leslie and Jay purchased the camp, they put the original copy of this letter in a frame and have it on a stand in the entrance to their cottage. Leslie and Jay wanted to make sure this was included in this book. I was so glad I could do so!

Cohen's Villa
On Beautiful Lake Champlain
Summer 1973

To Our Valued Clients,

    Cohen's Villa on the beautiful Lake Champlain in the heart of the Adirondacks has officially opened for the season. Your hosts, Fran and Bill, have plans for a great season.

    We will again have numerous activities, including boating, jogging, and hiking. You can again enjoy our excellent cuisine: steaks, lobster, caviar, and shrimp in season. This is not the season.

    For our Weight Watchers guests, we have hired a new chef (actually the same chef fifteen pounds lighter and with a new hairdo).

    We will again have a baby-sitting service and a special keep-fit program for expectant mothers.

    You can again enjoy the privacy of our cottage. (What privacy!)

    By special request, our social director Bobbie will be back this season to keep everyone busy and happy. (Whose request???)

    Our rates will be the same as last year, as we are anxious to maintain the high-class clientele we have always had. So please make your reservations early…and welcome back to COHEN' S VILLA ON THE LAKE.

Your hosts,
Fran and Bill

Awards

In May, someone in the writing class suggested that the topic for June would be "Awards."

I thought to myself, "How can I write on the subject of awards?" Here I am—88 years old—and I never even received a plaque or a trophy or a medal. Since I was never a Girl Scout, I never even received a Girl Scout pin. For a few minutes, I felt deprived. But then again, in our lifetime, we are rewarded in so many different ways, and some are more important than others are.

I was so pleased when my husband received the Liberty Bell Award, which included a plaque we hung on our wall, for his unselfish service to the community. I am always so proud when my children and grandchildren receive plaques and trophies for being outstanding in various activities. So, I guess I did something right, and I've been rewarded.

Time and time again, I have read articles where women complain that their husbands do not remember their birthdays and anniversaries with cards and gifts. My husband Bill gives me cards and gifts for only special occasions, so I'm not complaining, and he is my best friend. On our fifth anniversary, he surprised me with a five-"carrot" ring. The problem was that he could not afford a five-carat ring, so he bought one at the vegetable stand instead of at the jewelry store. At first, I was angry and disappointed, but then I thought I was lucky to have a husband with a good sense of humor. Many years later, he surprised me with a simple diamond wedding band. He tells me that I am as beautiful as I was as a bride. I tell him that he is lying like a rug but to keep lying!

Looking back, I feel the biggest rewards in my life are the love that my husband has given me and the joy that my children have given me. Our four caring children have given us eight grandchildren and two adorable great grandchildren of whom we are so proud.

I believe that life is like a carousel. It goes around and around. First, I was busy raising my children. Then I helped take care of my parents when they were incapacitated. Then I was busy helping with the grandchildren. Now we are full circle. Bill and I both have health problems and need help. Our children suggested that we come back north from Florida so they could take care of us. Now we are living in Coburg Village near them, which is a big help.

When I mention that Bill and I are married for almost sixty-six years and we worked alongside each other for many of those years in a retail business, people say that I deserve a medal. I do not need a medal. I've been rewarded with a wonderful family. That is a medal I wear in my heart, not on it.

Confidence

If anyone ever asked me who was the person who changed me from a person with no confidence to the person I am today, without thinking twice, I would say my husband Bill. I was so lucky to have him and to be married to him for sixty-eight years.

I grew up in New York City, the daughter of poor immigrants who did without so I could have a happy childhood. I did not realize that I grew up during the Great Depression. They showered me with love, surrounded me with loving aunts and uncles, and always regarded me as their *shayna, klayna maidelah*, their beautiful, sweet girl.

Despite their unconditional love, when I was around sixteen years old, I developed an inferiority complex. My mother was petite and had small features, but I looked like my father, who was short, on the heavy side, and had a prominent nose. To make matters even worse, I considered my two best girl friends as beautiful, with small features and nice figures. Next to them, I felt ungainly, fat, and unattractive. In addition, I was an average student who had to work hard to make good grades. Therefore, I envied anyone who was bright and found school less difficult.

For the first twenty-six years of my marriage, I was busy being a wife and a mother to our four children. Through those early years, I felt better about myself as I knew that Bill loved me, and he always told me how beautiful I was. When I was unhappy with my weight, Bill would say, "If I wanted a skinny wife, I would have married one." However, I still did not have the confidence in myself as I didn't regard myself as intelligent.

In 1966, Bill and I opened the Village Bazaar, a women's clothing shop. I was eager to help out. The children were now older with two already out of the house. At first, Bill asked me to help him type some business letters. "Bill, I can't do that!" I told him. "I haven't typed for over thirty years!" Bill said, "Just put your hands on the typewriter, and it will come back to you." I was surprised to realize that I knew where all the letters were on the keyboard, and the whole rhythm of typing came back to me quickly. Moreover, I found out that I loved to type because now I was doing it for our own business, not for a teacher or a boss.

As I had studied bookkeeping in high school, Bill encouraged me to take over bill paying for the store's merchandise and services. Again, just like the typing, my old skills came back quickly, and I loved "working the books." With his help, I learned how to do the payroll.

Bill convinced me that I would be an excellent salesperson, and since I knew the customers better than he did, an excellent buyer of store merchandise. As the business grew, we became business partners, working side by side. When Bill had to go to New York City for buying trips, I loved going with him as we combined business with pleasure. We went to the buying houses to pick out merchandise during the day, and we went to shows and restaurants at night.

I did not realize how much I had learned until my son Jay came home after his freshman year at Union College in Schenectady, New York. He had just completed a three-credit introduction to business class and began peppering me with questions regarding the way Bill and I ran our businesses. "Sunny boy," I told him, "your father and I have been running a business since before you were even born. We learned this by the seat of our pants, which is better than any business course they teach at your fancy school." That was a lesson in humility for Jay and a boost in confidence for me.

As I took over more and more of the bookkeeping at the store and spent time on the floor selling clothes, I became more conscious of what I was eating and lost twenty-five pounds. Knowing what I had learned about fashion and clothing, I dressed to flatter my figure and started using more make-up. At 56 years old, I got my ears pierced so I could wear nicer earrings. Bill also made me feel better about myself by continuing with his loving comments, such as "You are as pretty as the day I married you." With Bill's help, I had become a confident, attractive career woman.

Looking back at my life from the ripe old age of 93, I feel that I have accomplished so much, personally and professionally. My biggest accomplishment is being a mother of four children who all graduated college and had wonderful careers. They are good people and, as adults, they have always been there for Bill and me. They have blessed us with eight grandchildren and five great-grandchildren. I'm so proud of them all. Most importantly, they are proud of what their father and I accomplished in our lifetimes.

Even though I was never had a cheerleader's figure, or I never was the valedictorian of my class, I feel I have done well for myself and have had a very good, happy life. Much of my confidence comes from the love and trust Bill instilled in me.

Eleanor Roosevelt

O ur family always thought that Eleanor Roosevelt was one of the outstanding first ladies. Although Eleanor lived a sheltered life in a rich and prominent family, at seventeen years of age, she chose not the life of a debutante but preferred to work in a settlement house in Delancey Street to help the poor and disadvantaged. My mother, who was born in 1884, the same year as Eleanor, was working in a factory earning $3 a week. Therefore, my mother thought that Eleanor was wonderful in that she was a champion for people like herself, a poor immigrant from Russia.

Eleanor had a very sad childhood. When her parents married, they were a dazzling couple. Her mother Anna Hall was a beautiful debutante, and her father Elliot was a brother of Teddy Roosevelt. Their happiness did not last as her father was an alcoholic and her self-centered mother was disappointed that Eleanor was not beautiful. They made Eleanor feel unloved and ugly. Many tragedies followed. Her mother died at 34 years of age, and Eleanor and her two brothers were sent to live with Grandma Hall. Her brother and father died soon after.

When Eleanor returned from boarding school in England, she was delighted to be courted by her cousin Franklin Roosevelt. The first seven years of her marriage were happy ones. They were blessed with one daughter and four sons. Eleanor was devastated, therefore, when she discovered that Roosevelt was having an affair with Lucy Mercer, his secretary. Eleanor offered to get a divorce, but her domineering mother-in-law interfered. "If you

divorce, I will disown Franklin. Also, it will ruin his political career." So, their strange and in-name-only marriage continued. At times they were close when they had things in common, mainly in ways to help people through the Depression and the war.

Roosevelt, who was elected four times, spent more years in the White House than any other president. Their years in the White House were hectic. President Roosevelt was working very hard to end the war sooner. Eleanor was concentrating on making life for the folks at home and in the military easier.

Although Eleanor was busy with her own life, it was difficult for her to see her husband surrounded by beautiful and stylish women. Roosevelt spent a lot of time with the beautiful Crown Princess Martha of Norway, who had come to the United States with her children until the war ended. After President Roosevelt died, Eleanor was terribly upset to learn that the president had resumed his affair with Lucy Mercer many years earlier and was with her when he died.

Since President Truman thought Eleanor was very bright, he asked her to be a delegate at the United Nations. President Harry S. Truman later called her the "First Lady of the World" in tribute to her human rights achievements. Before Eleanor passed away, she told her children that she forgave Franklin for his affair with Lucy Mercer. She would light up when she spoke of Franklin and only thought of the good times she had with Franklin and her children. She died in 1962.

Modern Inventions

Two very distinct conversations with my grandchildren brought home the fact that they were far ahead of me in terms of the ways of the modern world. I also realized that our grandchildren take all the new ways of life for granted.

When our grandson Adam was six years old, he was playing in the sand on the beach. I asked him if he was building castles. Adam replied, "No,

Grandma, I am building condos and shopping malls."

Many years later, Grandpa and I were still spending summers in the old cottage on Lake Champlain. Our eight-year-old granddaughter Marissa saw me washing dishes. She said to me, "Grandma, don't you have a dishwasher?"

Grandpa and I had a very different, simpler life before all the inventions that make life easier. For example, before we had a modern refrigerator, everyone had an ice box. During the summer, the ice man would walk up two flights of stairs with the ice, for which my mother paid fifteen cents. There was a pipe that ran from the top to the bottom of the ice box. The pipe dripped the melted water into a pail that had to be emptied every day. I was delighted when we got a new modern refrigerator in 1925, when I was around eight years old.

Other "new" inventions in my lifetime include the following:

Invention	**Year**	**My Age**
Radio	1926	9 years old
First talking picture	1927	10 years old
First telephone	1929	12 years old
First automatic washer and dryer	1954	37 years old
First dishwasher	1965	48 years old (Manually connect to sink)
Personal Computer	1972	65 years old. Grandpa and I were retired and never learned how to use it.
Cell Phone	2000	73 years old. I never learned how to use it. Besides, the volume never was loud enough for me to hear it!

I always said I was born too soon!

Grandma Fradel's Thoughts, Sayings, and Advice

- When I was a little girl, I would say the following, "Mom, you married my father, and I have to marry a stranger."

- Eat well when the children are young as you need all your energy to take care of them.

- In order to strengthen your chances of marriage, remember the following: Why buy the cow when the milk is free?

- In order to strengthen your marriage, remember the following: If you don't feed your husband at home, he will go out to eat in a restaurant.

- When I was a young lady and dating, my parents prayed that I would meet someone with the same religion as ours and be handsome and rich. When I met Bill, he was Jewish and handsome. Two out of three is not too bad.

- After seeing *Gone with the Wind*, Bill proposed to me. He thought I was as pretty as Scarlett O'Hara. I thought Bill was as handsome as Rhett Butler. Of course, I said yes.

- In 1940, when we got married, we went on our honeymoon after the wedding, not before!

- Fortunately, Bill and I were happily married for 68 years. When I tell anyone that I was married for 68 years, they ask, "How many husbands?"

- My best advice to women of today: After you are married and busy with your children, be a loving wife. Your husband is your best friend.

- Respect your husband, and he will respect you.

- Dad bought me some cologne for Chanukah. I was so surprised and pleased. He told the salesgirl that he wants something for his 70-year-old wife who acts like 35. I didn't give him anything but aggravation.

- Dad started a new job today (March 19,1985) Hope it works out well. He got all dressed in a shirt and a tie. To me it felt like the last child in the house started school. If it works out, I told him to ask for vacation pay, a retirement plan, and maternity leave.

- I used to worry about silly things like why I could not master mah jongg at 70 years old. Then I realized that lots of these girls have been playing for 30 or 40 years. The same thing happened with yoga. I started it at 67 and expected to be in the Olympics at 70. I learned to accept myself.

- The men [at Hawaiian Gardens] are just a bunch of kids. Sunday morning, they start calling to plan the golf game. They remind me of my grandson Adam's friends calling, "Can you come out to play?" Then one does not want to play with this one. The only difference between them and the grandchildren is that these "boys" are grey and gold and have big tummies.

- We have the same problems with the ladies. When we plan setting up tables for 10 for condo affairs, this one doesn't not want to sit with that one. The only way to settle it is to have 50 tables for 50 couples. And you young folks want to live to a ripe old age. Prepare for it. Have hobbies and *save your money*.

Marilyn's Eulogy for Dad

In November 2008, my father, who had been in declining health for several years, was hospitalized for congestive heart failure. Mom, Dad, and I discussed kidney dialysis to prolong his life, but we all realized that at his age and in his condition, that was not the best medical route to take. We knew it was just a matter of days before we would lose him.

This was the eulogy I read at his funeral:

Thank you all so much for coming today to honor our father. We have been so fortunate to have our father in our lives for so many years. Bill Cohen was a wonderful man. He is leaving us with wonderful gifts and memories, some that I would like to share with you today.

First, our father gave us the gift of an appreciation for education and learning. He loved to read, and he passed this love onto his children by filling our home with books. As children of the Depression, neither of our parents had the opportunity to obtain a college degree. They were determined that each of their children would have that chance. As a result, all four of us were given a college education, quite a feat when tuition was probably about 25% of Dad's salary. His children all married individuals who also valued education and lifelong learning. He also gave us an appreciation for the value of using that education to benefit others through their careers and through community service.

The most important gift our father has given us is a deep appreciation for family. My father measured his success not by how much money he had in the bank but how much love he gave and was given to him by his family. He was blessed with a loving, enduring sixty-eight-year marriage to our wonderful mother. He was blessed with four loving children who have grown into caring, responsible, adults who have full, happy, and productive lives. He was blessed with his children's spouses who were never "in-laws," for they loved our father and mother as much as they loved their own parents. My father was blessed with eight wonderful grandchildren and their spouses who have given him so much pride and happiness. Our father was blessed with four great-grandchildren and the knowledge that another one was on the way. When you add in the love of all the members of our extended family—and my father had by his definition the largest extended family in the world—Dad was the richest man to have ever lived.

Our father leaves us a lifetime of memories through our family stories that thankfully have been captured in my mother's writings. We have wonderful memories of our home in Keeseville, a huge, rambling house that was often filled with relatives and friends gathered around a huge oak dining room table. We have the memories of growing up on Lake Champlain, having a beach a five-minute drive from our house, and having the chance to spend time in a series of boats that more often than not were either out of gas, out of oil, or out of luck. In 1966, Dad fulfilled a lifetime dream when he got my mother's blessing to purchase a summer cottage on Lake Champlain. For thirty-three years, the cottage was the family summer gathering place for all the children and grandchildren, and the source of numerous "Dad" stories.

Once they retired, Dad and Mom spent more and more of their time in Florida. In 2006, upon the children's insistence, my parents moved to Coburg Village to be closer to the family. We are grateful for the gift of these past two and a half years, where our parents have been surrounded by our huge extended family, by many old and new friends, and by the Congregation Beth Shalom community that have so warmly embraced my parents.

Finally, my father gave us the gift of his last days. My father was lucid and aware to the very end. Hours before his passing, he used his last bit of strength to say goodbye to his family, either in person or by phone: "I love you, I will miss you, all my love."

Three days before he passed away, my father asked me to promise him two things. The first was that all of us children were to take care of Mom. Dad, you have that promise, although right now I think she is taking care of us. The second promise was that we were not to shed any tears. That, Dad, is a promise we cannot keep. But we *can* promise that the majority of our tears will not be tears of sadness for our loss but tears of joy for the wonderful life you have lived and loved and shared with us.

Dad, we love you, we will miss you. All our love. *Marilyn*

Julie Shapiro's Eulogy for her Grandfather, Poppy Bill

A year and a half ago, while driving to Utah, Sam and I called Poppy Bill and Grandma Fran. Poppy Bill answered the phone first—a rare occurrence. "Hi Grandpa!" we said, "Where's Grandma?" "Eh!" he said. "She's out chasing men!" And then something like, "She never lets me talk, so I'm glad you called now."

Over the years, conversations with Grandma and Grandpa have ranged in subjects from the weather to jobs, to Colorado wildlife, to the food at Coburg Village, to favorite movies, to politics, to my car's mileage and Grandpa's scooter's maximum speed. And always, there were Grandpa's memorable one-liners. "How are you, grandpa?" I would always ask. And he would always respond, "Eh! I can't complain. When you're 94, you have different aches and pains than you had when you were 93."

Most importantly, we'd talk about family. It was his love of his family that put the joy in Grandpa's voice when we spoke to him and the twinkle in his eye when we saw him. With the news of each new birth or marriage, Grandpa would proudly update the family count: 23, 24, 25… "My family just keeps growing!" he would say. In my last call with Grandpa the night before he died, he and Grandma excitedly announced that his grandson David and his wife Shannon were expecting their first child.

When I first introduced my future husband Sam to Grandpa at Michael's Bar Mitzvah, Grandpa told him, "In our family, it's not about what religion you are; it's about how you treat each other." This idea that a family is more than blood—that it is about loving and caring relationships—this is the legacy that Poppy Bill leaves with us after a remarkable 94 years of life and 68 years of marriage. And though his children

Julie and Sam with Grandma Fran and Poppy Bill

and grandchildren have spread far and wide from the camp on a lake that first brought us all together, we remain connected by the relationships that were first fostered there.

A few months ago, I picked up my brother Adam at the Denver airport, and we drove the two and a half hours back to my house. We arrived late at night, and as I pulled into the quiet setting of my mountain home, I unexpectedly and acutely felt as though I were arriving at Lake Champlain as my family used to do on similar dark summer nights many years ago. When I shared this with Adam the next morning, he told me that he had felt the same way. This mutual emotion was more than a coincidence; it was, I believe, an inevitability arising from the power of shared experiences that, although long past, remain very much important and very much alive.

And so it is that while Poppy Bill himself never traveled west of the Appalachians, his keen sense of humor, his love of his family, the values he instilled in it, and the memories he created with it have traveled from coast to coast, from the Adirondacks to the Appalachians to the Rockies, to the Sierras, and to the desert southwest.

In this season of Thanksgiving, I am thankful for the wonderful times spent with Grandpa, and I look forward to the many occasions we will all spend together remembering and honoring him.

Mom's Contribution to Her Writing Group December 2008

One of the most exciting days of my life was the day I married Bill on August 20, 1940. Sixty-eight years later, it is going to be very difficult to go on without him. We were fortunate to be together in a good marriage.

A few weeks before he died, Bill said the following, "After I am gone, I do not want you or the children to cry for me. Instead, be thankful for the wonderful life we had. We were blessed with four children and their spouses, eight grandchildren and their spouses, and four great grandchildren."

Bill's only regret was that he never completed college. He was so proud that all his four children and grandchildren graduated college with bachelors, master's, and even doctorate degrees. Three graduated Phi Beta Kappa. In fact, I had to stop Bill from bragging.

Bill felt that he had a good life. Although he was born and brought up in New York City, he loved living in a very small town in Upstate New York. He enjoyed being in the retail business. I worked with him for over twenty years. We loved going to New York City on our buying trips for the store. At night we would eat at nice restaurants and take in Broadway shows.

Bill enjoyed being active in community service. He was a member of the Keeseville school board, president of the local Chamber of Commerce, and belonged to many other organizations. He was even Lieutenant Governor of the Kiwanis for New York State in the 1960s.

One of the smartest moves we ever made was buying a very rustic cottage on the New York side of Lake Champlain, where the whole family enjoyed swimming, boating, and taking walks.

After retiring, Bill and I spent over twenty-three years living in a condo in Florida. We were snowbirds for sixteen years, the best of both worlds. We loved to have our children and grandchildren visit us.

Beside his family, Bill will be missed by many, as he had a very sunny disposition. He was an optimist. If things were not good today, he always said tomorrow would be better. He had a sense of humor. For example, I had my hair done every Friday morning. When I returned from the beauty parlor, he would say, "Couldn't she take you today?" He would also ask if I heard any gossip. If I said there was no gossip that day, he said, "Why do you pay her?"

Bill always made me feel good about myself. When I gained weight, I wasn't happy. But he said, "If I wanted a skinny wife, I would have married one." And I especially loved it when he told me I was as beautiful as the day we married.

I can't express how much I will miss the handsome guy I married sixty-eight years ago. He will always be the love of my life.

Mom's Letter to Bill
Three Months After His Passing

Dearest Bill,

I thought that I would write you to tell you that all the children and I miss you and also to tell you that on February 27, 2009, we moved to another apartment in Coburg Village Number 925. Wherever I go, you also go in spirit.

Since the economy is not the best, I decided to downsize. Our large brown sofa looks lovely in front of the bay window in the new apartment. The rest of the furniture fits beautifully into the living room and bedroom. I especially am enjoying the location of the apartment as it is much nearer to Coburg's dining room and main entrance.

As for myself, I sit in your La-Z-Boy recliner watching CNN on television. I also sleep on your side of the bed so that I can feel closer to you.

When you said goodbye to all the family, you asked all of the children to take good care of their mother. They listened. They are doing a terrific job. I could not have moved without Marilyn's help as she did all the

packing before the movers arrived and then unpacked. All the children are always there for me, calling me frequently and planning on visits.

I miss you.

Your loving wife,

Fran

Adventures in Cooking

Once Bill and I were retired, we had more time to cook. One evening, since it was raining and cold, I asked Bill if he would enjoy chicken soup and *kneidlach* (matzoh balls). Instead, he said how about making *kreplach* (Jewish meat-filled dumplings). I told Bill, "You know how I feel about kreplach."

My aversion to kreplach goes back to when Annie, Bill's mother, came to visit our home in Alburgh, Vermont. Grandma Annie decided to make her son one of his favorite recipes, kreplach cooked with Karo syrup. The only problem was that I was pregnant with Laura, and the sweet kreplach made me even more nauseous.

The next time I decided to make kreplach, it was a disaster. After I spent hours in the kitchen, Bill told me that he didn't like them. "They are not as good as my mother's," he told me. So, I made up my mind never to make Grandma Annie's favorite recipe again.

It had been over 50 years since my first attempt, but the weather was terrible, and we had nothing else to do. I had all the ingredients in the house, including eggs and flour I had bought on sale. Besides, Bill said that he would help me. If they came out good, I could take credit. If they didn't, I could always blame him.

Bill insisted that we not change the recipe, which called for three eggs and one cup of flour. It didn't roll out with just one cup of flour, but we kept adding more until we had used at least two cups. The recipe said to cut the dough in 2-inch squares, but that seemed like too much work. I decided the recipe would work better by making circles in the dough with a glass.

Soon, Bill and I got into a nice rhythm. I made the circles, and Bill put the meat in the middle and pinched the edges. Then we fried the kreplach in vegetable oil

In the middle of cooking, we both complained of backaches. The kitchen counters, the kitchen floor—even Dad and I —were covered with flour. Besides, we had a sink full of dishes. Then we burst out laughing. Was it worth it?

The kreplach didn't come out as good as Grandma Annie's, but we had a lot of fun. I decided that I did not plan to make kreplach for another 50 years.

Once we moved to Coburg, we made breakfast and lunch in our condo. Each night, we ate in the huge dining room that offered five course meals. But they couldn't make everything we like, including chicken soup with matzoh balls.

Traditionally, chicken soup with matzoh balls is served on

Shabbos and Jewish holidays. Since my family enjoyed that soup so much, we had it all year. We knew that not only is chicken soup delicious but is also good for you. Known as "Jewish penicillin," doctors—especially good Jewish doctors—recommended it when you had a cold. We always added a few fluffy matzoh balls to the enjoyment. It was my husband Bill's favorite soup.

The chefs at Coburg Village were very creative and made all kinds of delicious soups: Italian Wedding, French Onion, even Russian borsht. But no chicken soup with matzoh balls! During the first two and half years we lived in our independent living facility, we were never served matzoh ball soup. Often the chef would stop by our table to inquire how we were enjoying our dinner. Bill would usually say, "Everything is very good. But when are you having chicken soup with matzoh balls?"

One Sunday, after Bill had passed away, I read the week's menu for the Coburg dining room. I was pleasantly surprised to see that on Wednesday the soup would be matzah ball soup. The day had come. The dining room was finally honoring Bill's request. The sad part was that Bill was not here to enjoy it.

Eulogies for Mom

After Dad's passing in November 2008, Mom continued to live in Coburg Village. She grieved silently, but as she told me many times, "One must adapt to life's changes, and I must learn to live without my dear Bill." She lived a full life the next two and a half years, dancing at her granddaughter Marissa's bat mitzvah, taking advantage of all that Coburg had to offer, and visiting with friends and family. She continued writing, and many of the stories in this book were written during that time.

On December 21, 2010, four days after I retired, I took Mom to a doctor's appointment. On the way home, we stopped for lunch. I was about to take out my credit card when I realized I had forgotten my wallet at home. Mom, upon hearing this, laughed and claimed that she would have to take me out now that neither Larry nor I were working.

That night, Mom called me to tell me that she had chest pains and had called the EMTs. I rushed over to the apartment as she was being loaded onto a stretcher. At the hospital, the doctor told me that Mom had had a heart attack and may not make it through the night. Fortunately, she survived, and we were able to take her home under hospice care. Her last months were filled with visits from children and grandchildren around the country as well as her many, many friends and relatives.

Ten days before her passing, Mom had a stroke. At one point, her wonderful hospice nurse assured Mom that she still had many good days in front of her. "No, I miss my Bill," she told the nurse and me. "I want to be with him." She slipped into a coma and passed away three days later on March 2, 2011. Mom was buried next to her beloved husband. She was just over 93 and a half years old. What follows are two eulogies read at her funeral.

Marilyn

Laura's Eulogy for Mom

Thank you for coming today to honor our mother.

I went off to college and came home during Thanksgiving break cursing like a sailor. When my mother started cursing. I told her that I never heard her swear like that before. Her answer to me was that since I had gone to college, and she had not, she wanted to benefit from my education.

Mom always had time to help us with homework, go to our sporting events, and sit through our recitals and concerts. During my sophomore year at college, she came to visit me and stayed in the dorm. She stayed up half the night sitting on the floor playing bridge with me and my friends.

The age span between me and Bobbie was 13 years, which saw many cultural changes. Mom changed with them.

Two weeks before passing away, she was watching the Grammy Awards with Marilyn. Mom had a little bit of difficulty with Lady Gaga, but she thought Justin Bieber was quite talented.

Laura's favorite picture of Mom

Mom loved the beach, but one had to drive to get there as it was three miles outside of town. Mom had never learned to drive. In 1954, she was determined get her license if only to go to the beach. Once she got her permit, she asked Dad to give her a lesson. They got in the car in the driveway, and he had her start the car. He told her to put it in reverse and back up. At the end of the driveway where it meets the street, he told her to put the car in drive and to pull up in the driveway. Then he told her to turn off the car, and he got out and went back into the house. That was the last time she relied on Dad for a lesson. She called Mr. Anderson, the school's driver's education teacher and a friend, to teach her.

Mom had to take her driving test three times. The first time she couldn't park. The second time she went through a red light. The third time she got the same inspector. Driving through the streets of Plattsburg, she went through a red light. The inspector asked her what color the light was. She turned to him, said it was green and then drove right onto the courthouse lawn. The inspector told her he was passing her because he never wanted to drive with her again.

Mom never was the best driver. She was barely five feet two inches tall; Dad was almost six feet. However, Mom never bothered to move the seat up in the car. As a result, she could barely reach the gas and brake. She also was hesitant, which meant she often drove too slowly for the traffic. This did not stop her. From the day she got her license, she enjoyed filling up our station wagon with kids, towels, beach balls, food, and, beginning in 1955, a playpen and other needed baby paraphernalia for Bobbie.

Mom was not impulsive except in one instance. In 1966 she and Dad went to look at a cottage thirty minutes from our home that was for sale. It was an idyllic setting. The log cabin cottage overlooked Lake Champlain. When Dad asked if they should consider buying it, she immediately agreed. Mom always said it was one of the best decisions they ever made. Ask any of the grandchildren their favorite memory, and they will tell you it was being at the cottage.

Julie Shapiro's Eulogy for Grandma Fran

In recent years, my grandmother had many pastimes—including reading, writing, visiting with friends and family, keeping up with current events and politics, and listening to Sinatra and show tunes on her iPod. And of course, there were the word search puzzles, an addiction of sorts fueled by WonderWord and the Daily Gazette.

Today I find myself searching for words, words commensurate to the person that we all remember Fran Cohen to be. She was a beloved wife, mother, grandmother, great grandmother, sister, cousin, aunt, and friend. She was a businesswoman with a savvy eye for style and a meticulous mind for bookkeeping. She was a

Julie and Grandma Fran

hostess of enormous generosity, constantly opening her relatively small (and thin-walled) lakeside camp to her large family—as well as their friends, their pets, their jigsaw puzzles sprawling across her treasured oak table, and their abundant appetites.

She was an admirer of historic women—Eleanor Roosevelt was a favorite subject—and she read and recounted their biographies with passion. She was also a champion of the "modern" woman, taking great pride in her career, encouraging her daughters and granddaughters to pursue their own, and checking in with my husband with some frequency to make sure that he was helping with the cooking.

She was an advocate of optimism and a believer in *b'shert,* Jewish for "it was meant to be." She approached life's challenges with wisdom and wit. Upon my sudden loss of a certain Toyota Camry that had once journeyed from Florida to Colorado, she wrote me a letter of condolence, reflecting humorously on its long life and wishing that it might rest in peace.

Throughout her own experiences with illness and with loss, including the loss of her husband, my Poppy Bill, she always emphasized the blessings. She lived in the present and honored the past. And through her writings, she brought the past to life. She was a storyteller whose memoirs—full of history, humor, and tenderness—will always connect us back to her and to our family.

Among Grandma's legacy to all of us are *her* words, those written in her stories and in her letters, as well as those countless and wide-ranging conversations that are recorded only in our memories. Through them she revealed the great woman that she was and taught me about the woman I'd like to be, one filled with love, generosity, wisdom, wit, empathy, and a belief that we can create our own happiness in life by searching for the blessings.

As I search for words to describe the blessing of having Grandma Fran in our lives, I find an indelible image in my mind. It is one of a lake at sunset, the same lake that Grandma fell in love with during a beautiful sunset in the summer of 1966. She recalled in her memoirs that in that moment "the view was magnificent." When the camp was recently rebuilt, she wrote fondly, "The structure may be new, but the sunset will be the same."

In this time of loss, I am comforted that certain things will remain constant—the sunset over an Adirondack lake, and the memory of a woman who herself was magnificent, one who reflected back to all of us her light and her beauty and her goodness. Now that she has passed, the structure of our lives will indeed be new and different, but in our hearts, she will be the same.

Part Two:

Marilyn Cohen Shapiro

In August 2013, I began submitting stories to the (Capital Region, New York) *Jewish World.* Over the past eight years, I have written many articles on a wide range of topics. Some of my favorites, however, have centered on my parents and my huge, wonderful family and extended family. The stories that follow are ones built on memories of me and my three siblings growing up in the Cohen household in a big old Victorian home in Keeseville, New York; our spending time in the cottage on Lake Champlain, and, as the years sped by, taking on our own responsibilities as adults, parents, grandparents, and caregivers to our beloved Mom and Dad.

Marilyn

The Four Cohen Kids

It is a hot day in late June. I wait impatiently on the front porch of our old Victorian house in our small upstate New York town. The blue sedan finally pulls into the driveway. My father climbs out from behind the wheel. As I skip down the steps and run across the yard, Dad opens the door on the passenger side. My mother holds a bundle wrapped in pink. I gaze in wonder upon a full head of dark brown hair and an infant's face crunched up and bright red from crying. "Meet your little sister Roberta Jessica," Mom said quietly.

That was my earliest memory. I was four years old, turning five and starting kindergarten three months later. I was thrilled to be a big sister.

I was probably the happiest of the Cohen family that day. My sister Laura, upon hearing before her thirteenth birthday that another child was on the way, immediately weighed in. "Why didn't you consult with me first?" she demanded. When told she was not part of the decision-making process, she stated, "Well, if you think you have a built-in babysitter, you have it all wrong!"

Jay, who was nine, only wanted a brother. When Dad woke him the morning of June 25 to tell him he had another sister, he groaned, pulled the covers over his head, and went back to sleep. I am not sure if he gave the newest addition another thought.

And I am not sure how happy my parents were when they realized that they were to be a family of six. Dad barely made enough money managing a small store to support a family of five, much less another child. Mom was thirty-six, looking forward to putting her youngest in full-day kindergarten and having a life without diapers and bottles.

But from the moment Bobbie came home (Roberta Jessica would forever more be saved for formal documents), I was fascinated. When my mother filled up the old bathinette with water to bathe her, I was right there beside her to help. When she needed to be pushed in the carriage, I wanted to be the one holding the handles. And when Bobbie needed casts on her legs to correct weak turned-in muscles, it was I who watched over her in her crib, which was set up next to the twin beds in my room.

I have heard stories about older children being jealous of their siblings when they came home from the hospital. Children who resorted to tantrums. Children who wanted to know when the baby was going back to the hospital.

A five-year-old rode her bike up and down her street crying, "Does anyone want a little girl? My parents don't love me anymore!" But I never remember being jealous. She was my little sister, my live baby doll.

If there were any difficulties between us, it was probably because everyone who met Bobbie immediately fell in love with her. She was always smiling, always happy, always easy going. This was in stark contrast to me—moody, anxious, and often fearful. Little Miss Sunshine could charm her way into everyone's heart, a direct contrast to my Little Miss Worrywart personality.

And Bobbie was beautiful. I was chubby, with thick glasses that covered my only good feature, my blue eyes. On the other hand, Bobbie had dark hair, high coloring, freckles sprinkled across her nose, and eyes that rivaled Elizabeth Taylor's.

As we grew up, Bobbie and I continued to be inseparable. She was always part of my parties, my sleepovers, my bike rides. In every one of the few pictures we have of our childhood, Bobbie is always front and center, her smile lighting up the world. Years later, when I asked my mother what it was like to have a baby at thirty-six years old, she said, "Marilyn, I didn't raise her. You did!"

The four Cohen children are fortunate indeed. Whereas many of my friends have strained or non-existent relationships with their siblings and/or their spouses, we all have remained close—maybe even closer now that we all realize how life can change on a dime. When Bobbie called her siblings in 2007 to share the devastating news that she had breast cancer, our initial thoughts were "This can't be happening to our little sister." But it was her "Little Miss Sunshine" attitude that got her through surgery, radiation, chemo, and her recovery. When Laura had a stroke several years later, she often referred to Bobbie's spirit during her cancer ordeal and was determined to be as strong. She was and still is, our Big Sister.

One of my parents' favorite pictures of the four Cohen kids was taken just before Laura graduated high school. We are sitting on a couch in our house in Keeseville. Jay is sitting on the arm rest, followed in order on the couch is Laura, Marilyn, and then Bobbie. None of us were at our most flattering best. As a matter of fact, we all looked pretty silly. In a home with few family pictures, however, that particular one graced my parents' living rooms for the rest of their lives. We siblings all kidded our parents and each other, wondering "This is the best we ever looked?"

The evening after our mother's funeral, we pulled out that picture and laughed again at the "family classic." Taking charge of the moment, Bobbie's husband Emil posed us all on my family room couch with the four of us trying hard to duplicate our fifty-plus years-ago expressions. Then we took a more straightforward one, without the goofy grins.

Jay, Laura, Marilyn & Bobbie 1968

Jay, Laura, Marilyn & Bobbie 2011

We have continued the tradition. Each time we are together, whether it is at a bat mitzvah or a weekend reunion, we will line up— Jay, Laura, Marilyn, and Bobbie—snap a picture, and are grateful that the "Four Cohen Kids" are happy, healthy, and together again.

Remembering Dad on Father's Day 2018

Ten years ago this week, my father and I spent our last Father's Day together. In 2006, he and my mother had moved to an independent living facility in Upstate New York four miles from my husband Larry and me. Two years later, his health had deteriorated, and he passed away on November 20, 2008. People may remember Bill Cohen for his stores in Keeseville, his community service, his pride in his family. What I remember—and treasure—about Dad were the stories about him that my siblings and I share again and again. Many of them centered on boats, bugs, and bats.

Having spent summers as a child on Lake Champlain, my father always dreamed of owning a boat. In 1965, he purchased a pink indoor-outdoor that my mother immediately named *Nisht Neytik,* Yiddish for "not necessary." During the summer, Dad rented space on a public dock in Port Kent, five miles from our house. And each Sunday, Dad would coerce us all to take a ride if the boat was in working order. Unfortunately, the boat spent more time in the shop than in the water. And when it was in the water, Dad was always panicking about the weather or the gas situation. One time, we took a long ride out to a nearby island, and my father realized that we might not

From postcard circa 1964. "Nisht Neytik" is first boat on top left of picture.

have enough gas to return. We were nervous wrecks until we finally pulled back into our slot.

In 1966, my parents bought a cottage on Lake Champlain. Soon after, Dad purchased an outboard with slightly better reliability. Larry and I were married in 1974, and in 1975, we went up to the lake for Memorial Day. Dad gave Larry a pair of waders Dad had picked up second hand and asked my husband to put up the docks for the boat. Before Larry was knee deep, the waders, which were riddled with tiny holes, filled up with water. Think Lake Champlain in May, when the water temperature barely reaches 60 degrees. Larry never forgave him.

For the next several years, the boat was anchored either on the dock or on an anchor about 200 feet from shore. Dad still loved boating but only if the weather was perfect. For hours before we were supposed to go out, Dad kept his ear near the radio, which was set for the weather station. If there was the slightest chance of rain, he refused to go through with the ride. When we children (and eventually our spouses) were old enough to go on our own, Dad installed a CB radio in the outboard so he could check up on us every few minutes. In a blatant act of defiance, Larry would turn it off. Dad never forgave him.

As much as my father loved boats, he despised bugs. He kept a can of bug spray next to his favorite chair on the back porch of the cottage and used it frequently—and liberally— to kill any passing fly or wasp. When the Raid wasn't enough, he got an outdoor fogger, which he used with the same careless abandon that he used with the aerosol can. One beautiful summer night, my sister Laura was putting food on the table when my father passed by the outside of the open window with the fogger in his hand. A potent cloud of pesticide permeated the air. Laura never forgave him.

When the Raid and the fogger failed, Dad called in the Big Guns. One hot, buggy summer's day, he purchased an electric bug zapper and hung it on the limb of the huge oak in front of the cottage. As the sun set across the lake, we heard from inside the cottage a quick zap as the first bug hit the grid, then a second, then 10, then 20. Before we knew it, every bug between our cottage and Burlington five miles across the lake was headed for the bug zapper. It took about 30 minutes for the 10-foot machine to become completely clogged. So much for Dad's battle against the bugs. From then on, he stuck to fly swatters and Raid. Lots of Raid.

Dad was more successful with bats. The cottage was always a gathering place for the family. One summer weekend, Larry and I were in one bedroom; my sister Bobbie and her husband, Emil, were in another; and Laura was in another. In the middle of the night, I headed to the bathroom. As I reached for the toilet paper, I realized that a bat was sitting on the top of the roll. Trying not to wake anyone, I ran back into our bedroom and shook Larry awake.

"There's a bat in the bathroom!" I whispered.

Larry awoke groggily. "Wha...? " He climbed out of bed, checked out the bat in the dim glow of the nightlight and suggested we close the door and wait until morning.

"But what if someone else has to go to the bathroom?" I asked.

"What are you two doing?" Our whispered conversation had awakened Bobbie.

The bat, tired of squeezing the Charmin, flew out of the bathroom and began swooping through the cottage.

"Damn!" I cried.

By this time, Emil, Laura, and Mom were wide awake. Standing in the big open room, we watched the bat circle above us, all of us talking at once with suggestions of what to do.

"Hit it with the badminton rack!"

"How about a broom?"

"Does Raid work on bats?"

"How about the fogger?"

At that moment, my father, who can sleep through a five-alarm fire a block from our house—yes, he did. Keeseville, New York, Feb. 14, 1964. But I will save that story for another time—finally appeared in the doorway of his bedroom in his Hanes tee shirt and boxers. Without a word, he crossed the room, grabbed the fishing net that he kept in the corner explicitly for this purpose, and in one fell swoop, caught the bat in its web. He opened the front door, shook the frightened but still alive bat out of the netting, and came back into the cottage.

"Everyone now go back to sleep!" my father said.

Boat lover. Bug hater. Bat rescuer extraordinaire. But most importantly, My Dad. Whether he is with me or not, I will celebrate Father's Day in his memory with love.

The Gift of Reading

Shortly after my parents were married, their first argument was about finances. With an $18-a-week income as a salesclerk in Alburgh, Vermont, my father was spending up to $4 a week on magazines and books. My mother managed to curb his spending, but neither curbed their love for reading.

My parents were first-generation Americans, born of Jewish-Lithuanian immigrants. Children of the Depression, which squelched any hopes for education beyond high school, my parents compensated for their lack of opportunity with a legacy of literature: books, magazines, newspapers, and frequent trips to the libraries in the small towns of Vermont and Upstate New York where they raised their four children.

As a result, my siblings and I grew up in a house full of books. Two rooms had floor-to-ceiling shelves loaded with novels, second-hand encyclopedias, and American Heritage anthologies. My earliest memories were of sitting on my mother's lap as she read Golden Books to me. Birthdays and holidays always meant new books: *The Wizard of Oz*, *Shirley Temple Story Book*, and, in later years, the latest Nancy Drew, which my father would purchase in New York City on his buying trips.

When the books in our house weren't enough, one of my parents walked me to the small but well-stocked library around the corner from our house in Keeseville. An early reader, I soon graduated from the six-foot bookshelf stuffed with *The Cat in the Hat* and *Curious George* and moved onto the twelve-foot-high shelves with more challenging options. *Pippi Longstocking* and *Alice in Wonderland* were followed by Helen Keller's autobiography and *The Good Earth*. I would spend hot, summer afternoons in a green lounge chair on the side porch doing what I loved best: reading.

It was no surprise, then, that my four years of college focused on literature. I spent hours reading, discussing, and analyzing Shakespeare, Milton, Melville, and Hemingway. My literature course was not work: it was just a more academic extension of those leisurely afternoons in the green lounge chair.

That was my parents' heritage. Their rich love for literature was passed on to me, my siblings, and our grandchildren. It was the best gift they could have given us.

My Father The Designated Driver

A Father's Day memory: It is 1956. My father, Bill Cohen, is sitting behind the steering wheel of an idling sedan in the driveway of our house in Keeseville. Laura, Jay, and I are squirming in the back seat. He is smoking a Kent and listening to WEAV-AM out of Plattsburgh. He gives the horn an impatient tap to hurry along my mother, who is inside diapering Bobbie and pulling together last-minute items for our car trip. He honks again, more loudly. "Where is that woman?" he says. "We're going to be late."

For over sixty-five years, Dad was our family's self-appointed Designated Driver. Born and raised in Queens, Dad learned how to drive when he was fifteen years old at his grandfather's farm in Burlington, Vermont. In 1940, my mother, Frances Cohen, took her place in the passenger seat. By 1955, four children were filling up the remaining space.

Out of financial necessity, our family usually owned "gently used" cars. No matter how pristine they were when purchased, each vehicle soon lost the 'new-car' feel once our huge family—with an occasional dog along for the ride—took ownership.

These were the days before cars had safety features. No one wore seat belts; the baby sat on mother's lap; Dad's extended right arm held us back when we were forced to a sudden stop.

As the family grew, sedans gave way to station wagons. One or two of us children happily climbed into the back, where we bounced our way to a school function or the beach or a relative's house or even to visits to our grandparents in New York City, oblivious to any danger. Fortunately, Dad was an excellent driver. He was never involved in an accident. And his only speeding ticket was when—as he never let me forget—he was rushing home from a trip to Plattsburgh after I was car sick.

Not that he wasn't guilty of "pedal to the metal." In the 1960s, my father was elected coroner of Essex County, New York, a position he held for over twenty years. When he got the call from the state police that he was needed to investigate an unattended or suspicious death, Dad would rush out to his car, put the Essex County Coroner sign in his window, slap on his "Kojak" flasher on top of the car, and drive to the scene like a bat out of proverbial hell. If the call came in the middle of the night, one of us would often ride with Dad to keep him company. I remember sitting in the passenger seat while Dad careened through the back roads of Reber or Essex or Port Kent, praying one of the other three coroners in the county wouldn't have to investigate *our* untimely demise.

Soon after they retired in 1981, Dad and Mom began spending half the year in Florida. Each year in mid-October, they drove the 1500 miles to their condo in Lauderdale Lakes. The week before Memorial Day, they took the same route back. Although they eventually took the auto train to reduce driving time, Dad continued his reign as exclusive—and excellent—driver.

As he got into his eighties, however, his driving skills declined. His hearing was poor, his reaction times were slow, and he relied too often on cruise control so he wouldn't have to regulate the gas pedal. Concrete car-stop bumpers in parking lots saved many an eating place from becoming an impromptu drive-in restaurant. Still, Dad insisted on taking the wheel, promising to limit his trips to nearby restaurants and stores.

In 2005, while visiting Mom and Dad in Florida, Jay and his wife Leslie made plans for the four of them to go out to dinner. The usual fight ensued. "I'll drive!" Jay offered. "Absolutely not," Dad countered "You're my guest. *I'll* drive."

The route to the restaurant included a section on a multi-lane expressway. Dad was in the far-left lane when he suddenly crossed four lanes to get to the exit ramp. "We watched in horror from the back seat," Jay said. "Fifteen years later, I can still remember how Leslie's nails felt as she dug them into my arm until I bled."

After that incident, we children insisted Dad give up the car. We arranged for Mom and Dad to move into Coburg Village, an independent living near Larry and me that offered, among other amenities, transportation to stores and doctors' offices. They flew up to their new home, and Laura and Jay drove Dad's car to our house. Dad's Toyota would

105

stay safely in our driveway until Julie picked it up and drove it back to Colorado that summer.

For the next few months, Dad complained incessantly as to how we had taken away his independence. The day Julie came home to claim the Toyota, however, Dad pulled out of his wallet the registration AND an extra car key.

"You could have walked down the driveway and driven that car anytime you wanted to!" I said.

"I know," he said with a wink.

After that, Dad grudgingly accepted his place in the front passenger seat when either Larry or I drove. Six months before he passed away, Dad got a brand new shiny red mobility scooter. When I came over to have dinner that night in the Coburg dining room. Dad was already sitting on his new toy with a huge smile on his face. Mom and I followed him as he navigated his way down the long hallway to the open elevator door. Entering a little too fast, he gently hit the back wall. "I'm fine!" Dad said. "I got this! "

Of course, he was fine! My father was finally in the driver's seat again.

Remembering Mom on Mother's Day

Frances 'Fradel' Cohen was one special lady, and I was blessed to have her as my mother. She taught me many things during her long life, lessons that I hopefully will pay forward to my children.

Lesson One: There is always room at the table for more.

Six Cohens crowded around the kitchen table in Keeseville, but there was always room for more. Our school friends were always welcome. Salesmen coming through Keeseville on their Upstate New York route often joined us with a half an hour's notice. We had large Sunday lunches with relatives from Chateauguay and Brushton, and they often stayed late enough to catch a second meal before driving the hour or so back home. Much of our family lived in New York City, and their visits never lasted less than a week.

Mom & Marilyn 1951

When the number of people surpassed room in the kitchen, we always could pull out the oak table in the dining room that held about twenty. And the pot was always full. The Grand Union was less than a two-minute walk from our house, and we frequently did last-minute runs before it closed at 5:30 p.m. Besides, Mom always cooked for a family twice our size, and she always had ways to stretch the food, so everyone came away satisfied.

Lesson Two: Set an example for your children.

We rarely heard my mother swear. Once in a while, she would spit out a "damn" but that was the extent of our mother's four-letter-word vocabulary. There was one glaring exception. In December 1960, Laura came home for winter break from her first semester at SUNY Geneseo. She had learned a great deal in those first three months, and one lesson was how to curse. She colored her conversations with words that had never been heard in that old house in Keeseville. My mother listened but didn't reprimand Laura. Instead, she peppered her own conversations with profanities. Laura, shocked, said to Mom, "You never curse! What happened?"

"We sent you off to college so you can get a good education," Mom replied. "We're spending a lot of money for that education. So if my college-educated daughter can swear like a drunken sailor, so can I."

Laura never swore in front of Mom again.

Lesson Three: You are never too old to pursue your dreams.

My mother was the family storyteller. Give her an opening, and she would regale any audience with stories of her grandparents' and parents' lives in Russia, of her early years of marriage to "My Bill," of their life in small towns and smaller apartments in the North Country, and of raising four children. Soon after moving from Florida to an independent living facility near us, my mother joined a monthly writing group at Coburg. Initially she was concerned that her stories, which she had always shared aloud, would come across as unpolished and boring in written form. She was delighted when her fellow authors told her that she had a natural flair for storytelling. By the time she passed away in 2011, she had written pages and pages of family history.

Just like Grandma Moses, my mother found out she had an undiscovered talent late in life. She always used it as a life lesson for us. "You are never too old to pursue your dreams," she told us. "Look at me! I became a writer in my eighties!"

Lesson Four: Changing with the times is sometimes a good thing!

When I lived in upstate New York, I was a member of the Hadassah Book Group, and on occasion my mother would join me at the meetings. One month, the selection was *This is How I Leave You,* Jonathan Tropper's hilarious account of a dysfunctional Jewish family's week of sitting shiva.

At synagogue one evening, I mentioned to a friend that my mother would be attending the meeting.

"Your mother is reading that book?" she exclaimed. "Why, it's filled with sex scenes and obscenities. I am surprised you even told her about the novel."

"My mom is fine with it," I said. "She's pretty cool!"

At that moment, my mother joined us. "Lee is surprised you are reading Trooper's book," I explained. "She thinks it's too racy for you."

"I'm loving it," said my mom. "In fact, I now know why I haven't been able to publish my stories. They're not racy enough. I am going to start adding colorful language and sex scenes. THEN maybe I could finally get in print!" Okay, so my sister couldn't swear back in 1960, but my mom could consider it fifty years later if it would advance her writing career! In the end, she didn't have to spice up her writing after all. After she passed away, I began writing for Jewish newspapers, and I shared several of her stories in print and on my blog. Best of all, her writing is in this book, **Fradel's Stories.** I know my mother is smiling from heaven.

Recently, my daughter Julie shared a memory of my buying her a gold dress for a middle school dance "I must have tried on ten or twenty dresses before we bought that one," Julie said. Even when she decided not to go to the dance, Julie tried on the outfit another ten or twenty times before she had me return it. "You always had patience for me for stuff like that," she concluded. "Thank you."

I didn't remember the story, but I was so grateful that Julie shared it with me. I wonder now if Mom would remember any if all the stories I shared above. But I know she would be grateful that I remembered, and that I love and miss her every day.

Our Home in Keeseville

Larry and I have lived in three homes in our almost 45 years of marriage. All three have been lovely, especially after we made them our home with our personal touches. None of the places we lived, however, could compare to the memories I have of the house with all its nooks and crannies in which I grew up.

In 1952, my parents moved within New York State from Potsdam near the St. Lawrence River to Keeseville on Lake Champlain. At the time, real estate was limited, so my father found the one house large enough to accommodate Mom, the three children, and a cat. It was an old but proud 1899 Victorian set on a pretty lot only a block from Pearl's, the department store my father managed.

The front entrance to the house required climbing five steps to a small porch and a front unheated vestibule. A large oak piece with a mirror graced the right side; an old makeshift storage closet on the right side of the door held all the outerwear needed for the four seasons of Upstate New York.

Five Vine Street, Keeseville, New York

Beyond the foyer, a large living and dining room stretched out across the entire front of the home, with an oak arch dividing the two rooms. Guests often joined us around the large oak table in the dining room for Rosh Hashanah, Thanksgiving, and Passover.

The blue sectional in the living room came from Pearl's warehouse, not close to what my mother wanted, but what we could afford on my father's small manager's salary. I have memories of sitting on my mother's lap on that scratchy couch, listening with my thumb in my mouth as she read me various Golden Books, including *The Brave Little Tailor* and *Dumbo*. A piano, first an ugly orange upright and, in 1963, a small baby grand, filled up the rest of the space.

Straight ahead from the front entrance was another door that opened into the kitchen. When the house was first purchased in 1952, it was the saddest room: one single light bulb hanging from the ceiling, outdated appliances, cracked linoleum floors, a pantry covered with cobwebs and—to the joy of our cat—filled with mice. The first room to undergo a complete transformation, the finished room had wood cabinets, a stove with a double oven, a large refrigerator, and enough space for hold a Formica-topped metal table with six matching chairs. Just below the clock on the far wall was the hole in the yellow linoleum. It was the forever memory of the day when I was eight years old and threw a fork at my older brother, Jay, my fairly violent reaction to his teasing. Thankfully, the fork just missed his head before lodging in the yellow tile wall covering. I don't remember getting punished.

In another fight I had with Jay, he twisted my arm when I refused to stop bouncing an orange against that infamous yellow wall. I passed out and hit my head on a radiator on the way down to the floor. Jay got grounded for two weeks.

A door on the left led to a small unheated vestibule where fresh milk was delivered for years and a set of wooden steps that led to our backyard and driveway. A door to the right of the kitchen led to the originally only bathroom with a wonderful claw-toothed bathtub. I remember splashing in the tub, refusing to wrap myself in Mom's waiting towel until every drop of water had drained out.

To the left of the kitchen was a small, dark room that became the office. Mom did the store's bookkeeping for Pearl's department store on the massive metal desk. The wall behind her was covered from top to bottom with bookshelves that held second-hand encyclopedias, cookbooks, history books from *American Heritage*, tons of children's books, and 75 rpm records ranging from classical masters to Frank Sinatra to Danny Kaye reading Hans Christian Anderson. A chair with a table lamp served as my own gateway to the joys of reading on my own.

A second door in the back of the kitchen led to an unfinished and unheated room which originally was used as a storage area. A back window provided access to a 30-foot clothesline that was tethered to the house on one end and to a large oak tree on the other end. Soon after we moved in, my parents converted the "shed" into a family room by adding insulation, paneling, and a tile ceiling. Two recliners faced the television, the one on the left my father's retreat after dinner every night he was home. Mom took the chair on the right, usually engrossed in a book while Dad watched Perry Mason—originals and reruns. We piled onto the couch along the radiator wall or onto the floor.

An enclosed staircase at the far-left end of the dining room led upstairs to a small hallway with the doors to the four bedrooms. The first on the left was my bedroom. A trapdoor to the attic—which was never accessed—provided a source of nightmares for me, as did the long, narrow closet that ran along the side of the room. When Bobbie was born in 1955, she slept in the crib and eventually the twin bed next to me. Outside of her breaking a ceramic squirrel that held my glasses and watch, I don't remember any fights occurring over our being "roommates" for the next five years.

The bedroom had a window that opened to a flat asphalt tiled roof. When our mother wasn't looking, we children took turns climbing out and sitting on that asphalt tiled roof. When we were very brave, we dangled our feet from the edge over the clothesline filled with sheets and clothing and, after Bobbie arrived, diapers. Sometimes conditions necessitated trips onto the roof. Jay was responsible for shoveling snow off it to avoid leaks onto the ceiling of the family room below.

Jay's room was next to mine. A large closet had been cut to make the second bathroom that required walking through his room to use. It gave me a chance to check out his stash of *Superman* comics. When he found out I had touched them, he tossed them all out, a decision he lived to regret years later when such comics sold for a very decent return.

Laura's room was next to Jay's. It held two twin beds with pink chenille bedspreads, a dresser, and a matching desk. As she was eight years my senior, I was in awe of the crinolines and poodle skirts that covered her floor and the make-up and costume jewelry that covered her dresser. When she left on a fall Sunday morning in 1960 to enter Geneseo State College, I asked my parents five minutes later if I could move into her room. My mother asked me to wait until at least the bed was cold. To make her feel better, I waited an entire 24 hours.

My parents' bedroom was a treasure trove of nooks and crannies. The huge closet had a secret shelf that I found out years later held the store receipts and cash brought home every Saturday night until Dad could make the deposit at Keeseville National Bank on Monday morning. The maple bedroom set, which my parents had purchased in 1940 with the "Zayde" inheritance, included a tall bureau for Dad and a long dresser for Mom. On the top was my mother's green jewelry box; a 1950 family picture of Mom, Dad, Laura, and Jay (and me—she was pregnant!); and a glass tray that held Evening in Paris, a package of Sen-Sen mints, and assorted buttons, pins, and change. At the foot of their double bed was a large oak chest filled with pillows and blankets. When emptied, it became a wonderful boat or train. A second "closet" was carved out of the tiny room that sat above the downstairs foyer. My mother's long, maroon bathrobe hung in that closet— when I wasn't taking it out to play dress-up.

The main basement was accessed from still another door in the kitchen. Fourteen wooden steps with no railings led to a warren of four rooms that held, respectively, the washer and dryer; the old coal furnace; the "pantry," which held extra canned food in case of a nuclear war, and, for many years, a train set; and a small room that held paint, Dad's tools, and, behind a thick wooden door, paints, and chemicals. A second basement, a root cellar, was under the family room and only accessible by a half door with a wooden peg for a lock in the back of the house. I remember on several occasions my brother Jay and I, along with a couple of neighborhood friends, opened the door that led to that dark space, where we lit magic snake pellets in the dirt. We quietly watched them uncoil, then turn black, and then turn to ash. Years later, when I shared this secret with my mother, she was shocked. "You could have burnt the house down!" she exclaimed.

Much changed over the 30 years my parents owned the house. The house's three porches, one on the side, one on the front, and one behind the kitchen, eventually succumbed to age; it was easier for my parents to remove than replace. The metal kitchen cabinets were replaced with wood; the bathroom and its claw-toothed tub was remodeled soon after I went to college; the downstairs got carpeting. In the late 1970s, Mom and Dad had the house sided in green vinyl, a definite improvement over the white chipped paint.

In October 1981, my parents sold the house and moved into their cottage year-round. Larry and I came the weekend of the move with Adam, who was three and a half, and Julie, who was six months old. Everything Mom and Dad wanted to keep had been moved to the cottage, where they took up full-time residency until they were able to retire and live in Florida half the year. The rest they had put in a U-Haul for us to sort through once we emptied the contents into our one-car garage. That was the last time I set foot in the house, even though we have driven past it innumerable times.

Like the last scenes in the movie *Titanic,* I often dream of the house and the memories it held for me and my family. And one day, I will have the time and courage to knock on the front door and introduce myself to the current residents—the same family that bought it from my family almost 30 years ago. I will ask if I can wander through my childhood home, and I will check all the nooks and crannies one last time—looking for traces of that brown haired, bespectacled child and her life in that old, nostalgia filled house.

Laundry Day

When one is looking for a home in today's market, one of the featured perks is the laundry room. Multi-functioning washing machines and dryers, fancy cabinetry, shining stainless steel sinks, and granite countertops appear to make Wash Day a joy. What a contrast to the way my mother handled the laundry in Upstate New York in the 1950s!

In 1952, my family moved into a two-story house in Keeseville that had been built at the turn of the century. Compared to the tiny "box" we had lived in Potsdam, the four-bedroom Victorian with its large living and dining rooms, ancient but large kitchen, office, a large unfinished room off the kitchen, and three (!) porches must have felt like a castle.

Our laundry room, however, was more like a dungeon. Out of necessity, the wringer washer had to be set up in the basement, a dark, damp room with dirt floors, old stone walls, and a small window that looked out to the crawl space under one of the porches. A single hanging bulb provided the only light.

With two adults, three children—including one in cloth diapers—and lots of company, my mother had plenty of laundry. The wonders of polyester and wash and wear were still several years away. Either clothes were dry cleaned or "put through the wringer." After a scare when my older sister Laura got her arm caught in the wringer mechanism, the old machine was replaced with a more modern top loading model. My mother must have thought she was in the lap of luxury.

Electric dryers had not yet found their way to Upstate New York, so all the wash had to be hung to dry. Mom carried the wet laundry up the steep basement stairs, walked through the kitchen and through the door to the back of the unfinished storage room. She opened a large window and hung the clothes on the thirty-foot clothesline that was attached by a pulley system. One end was attached to the house and the other end to an oak tree that marked the far-right corner of our property.

When the weather was good, sunshine and warm breezes quickly dried the sheets, pillowcases, towels, diapers, shirts, pants, dresses, and underwear that hung ten feet above our backyard. Mom would then pull the line of dry clothes toward the house, unpin the items, and pile them into waiting laundry baskets. The cotton fabrics would smell like fresh air and sunshine. They would feel more like stiff boards of wrinkled matzoh.

If an unexpected rainstorm came through, Mom would have to quickly pull everything off the line and hang them over available chairs and radiators to finish the process. During the long winter months, cold air poured into the unheated room as Mom, fingers red and raw, pinned the laundry to the line with the wooden pins. If the snow was too frequent, she resorted to hanging the laundry in the basement.

Almost everything had to be ironed. Mom filled an empty soda bottle with water and stuck an aluminum and cork sprinkling head into the top. She lay out each item of clothing on the kitchen table, sprinkled the material well, rolled it up, and placed it in a laundry basket. She let all the dampened clothes sit awhile so the moisture would be well distributed. If she was afraid of mildew, she stuck the clothing into the large freezer chest that was housed in the shed.

When she and the clothes were ready, Mom set up the ironing board in the kitchen, plugged in the iron, licked the tip of her index finger on her tongue, quickly touch its wet tip to the bottom of the iron to check the temperature, and then pressed the steaming metal plate into the fabric. Taking each damp, rolled piece out of the laundry basket, she ironed for hours while listening to the songs of Frank Sinatra, Patti Page, and Tennessee Ernie Ford on WEAV-AM out of Plattsburgh. The kitchen would be filled with the sound of sizzling clothes and the smell of hot metal against the damp cotton.

The laundry increased with my sister Bobbie's arrival three years after our move. By the time she was out of diapers, my parents had purchased a clothes dryer. Pink boxes of Dreft and plastic bottles of Clorox sat on a brown metal table between the two appliances, along with yellow bars of Fels Naphtha soap, stray buttons, and assorted pair-less socks. Despite the addition of the tumble dryer, Mom still often used the clothesline on beautiful upstate New York days as she loved the smell of sunshine and fresh air on the sheets.

There was still a great deal to be ironed, so my mother gave her children pressing lessons at an early age. Starting with relatively easy handkerchiefs and pillowcases, we soon progressed to pants ("Make sure the seams are straight.") to shirts and blouses ("Start with the back and progress to the front and sleeves.") to dresses ("First do the bottom skirt, pushing the iron gently but firmly up to the waistband.").

I don't recall my father ever helping with laundry his entire life, but my husband Larry has been by my soapy side since our apartment laundry room days. Once we moved into a house in Clifton Park, we set up an ironing board next to our washing machine and dryer in our basement/laundry area. To this day, he washes our bedding every week and does most of the laundry, including a weekly sheets and towel load. (Another reason I love him!)

Our Yes!-We're-Retired! Florida wardrobe doesn't require extensive pressing. No matter, at least twice a month, I pull out the steam iron and the twenty-year-old ironing board. I spread our shirts and blouses and pants and handkerchiefs one by one on the ironing board. I wet each item with distilled water from a plastic spray bottle, automatically lick my index finger on my tongue, quickly touch its wet tip to the bottom of the iron to check the temperature, and then press the steaming metal plate into the fabric. I hear the familiar sizzle, and I breathe in the distinct aroma of cloth and water and heat and traces of laundry detergent. I am happy knowing that our clothes will be pressed and ready to wear—just like my mother taught me sixty years ago.

Coming Up for Air: Swimming

As schools let out for the summer, children head to the beach or the pool. Fortunately, my own first experiences with swimming certainly did not seriously hurt my current enjoyment of the sport.

In 1952, my parents moved our family from Potsdam to Keeseville. Both were small upstate New York towns. But whereas Potsdam had a college, including the Crane School of Music, Keeseville was a fairly poor mill town. Soon after my father took over as manager of Pearl's Department Store, the business at Prescott's Lumber, the company that made wooden television cabinets, slowed as manufacturers moved to less expensive metal cases.

Our new home, however, had one major advantage. Keeseville was located less than four miles from Port Douglass, a lovely spot on Lake Champlain that offered a sandy beach with a diving raft a hundred yards offshore. My mother grew up within walking distance of Coney Island's beach and boardwalk and loved the water. She was determined to get her license so she could drive us to the beach herself during our summer vacations.

As we lived only a block away from Pearl's, my mother would walk me over to the store, hand me over to my father, and then drive away with Mr. Anderson for her weekly driving lesson. While Dad managed the cash register, I sat in a back corner of the old building, listening to 78 RPM records: Walt Disney's *Snow White and the Seven Dwarfs;* Brothers Grimm and Hans Christian Anderson stories read by Danny Kaye; James Thurber's *The Thirteen Clocks*. Mom passed her driver's test on her third try. Soon after, she got her license in the mail, and I got to take those special records home to listen again and again on our family photograph.

Every summer afternoon, weather permitting, Mom would pile all of us into the station wagon, along with whatever friends tagged along. We would happily bounce our seat-beltless way to the beach, nestled between towels, a couple of chairs, a cooler filled with snacks and drinks, and—once Bobbie was born—a playpen and a diaper bag. Once we got there, we dumped everything onto the sand. Mom would sit in a chair chatting with her friends as we ran into the usually freezing water. (This was Upstate New York, remember, where the water temperature ranged from sixty degrees in early June to a balmy seventy degrees by August.)

Laura & Marilyn at Port Douglass 1953

I remember the beach, but I also remember the day—I was probably four—that I waded in too far and found myself over my head. I frantically struggled in three feet of water, going under once, twice, three times. Luckily, a teenager who was standing near my dilemma, fished me out, and put me back on shore. Sputtering, scared, but safe, I ran back to our blanket.

"I drowneded!" I told my mother. "That's nice, sweetheart," my mother said and went back to her conversation with her friends.

In the years that followed, I, along with many of my friends, took swim lessons at Port Douglass. For six weeks a summer, we caught an 8 a.m. bus provided by the town to take classes taught by high school students. The four years of lessons are etched in my memory through the songs we would sing while being shuttled back and forth: *Wake Up Little Susie* (1957); *Tom Dooley* (1958); *Battle of New Orleans (1959); and Tell Laura I Love He*r (1960). We'd get home in time for lunch and often a second trip to the beach with Mom behind the wheel.

Around 1961, a swimming pool facility was built near Ausable Chasm. Our family obtained a membership, and we split our time between the sandy beach and the warmer waters of the pool. In 1966, our parents purchased a cottage on Willsboro Bay, across from Burlington, Vermont. We swam off our boat dock and off the small public beach adjacent to our property.

It was also during those summers in Willsboro that I learned how to water ski, resulting in one of the most embarrassing moments of my life. When I was sixteen, I was water skiing behind a boat driven by a very cute neighbor with his equally cute friend, who was spotting me. All of a sudden, I realized that I had lost the top of my two-piece bathing suit. I quickly let go of the tow line and submerged myself up to my neck in the middle of the bay. The two "Troy Donahue" twins brought the boat around to retrieve me. They somehow managed to hold their laughter as they handed me my aqua and white ruffled top—now missing their two back buttons—while I handed over my skis.

While in college, I occasionally swam laps in the university's athletic center, but my pool time increased exponentially once Larry and I had children. We joined a neighborhood pool four miles from our house. Adam and Julie played in the water with friends, and I caught a few laps during adult swim. They both took swim lessons and subsequently joined a swim team. We spent many a summer night with timers in our hands as Adam, Julie, and their teammates made their way back and forth the pool with their breaststrokes and freestyles and butterflies.

Larry was not much of a swimmer himself, but he insisted both children get their lifeguard certification. For several years, they got jobs life guarding at our town pools and at college pools. Julie spent two summers managing the pool at The Hole in the Wall Gang Camp in Connecticut, a resort for seriously ill children founded and sponsored by Paul Newman. Julie has fewer opportunities to swim—nearby mountain-fed Lake Dillon rarely gets above 63 degrees in the summer—she paddle boards. Adam still swims regularly in indoor pools near his San Francisco apartment.

In Florida, I swim in our neighborhood pool several times a week. The water is heated to 82 degrees, so warm for my Upstate blood that I have been known to do laps when the air temperature is under sixty degrees. I am a strong swimmer, gliding slowly but steadily back and forth in my lane for forty, fifty minutes without a break. But once in a great while, I inhale a mouthful of water, start choking, and lean on the side of the pool to catch my breath. For that short moment I remember once upon a time, I "drowneded," but I have lived to tell the tale.

The Sound of Music

For our family, three of the best gifts we ever received were an ugly orange spinet, a mahogany baby grand, and a walnut Yamaha upright. After the war, my parents and my two older siblings moved from New London, Connecticut, to Potsdam, New York, so that my father could help Uncle Eli, my mother's brother, with his clothing business. Housing was difficult to find in 1948, and my parents were left no option but to purchase a small ranch house on top of a frequently windy hill. Cramming the four of them into the two-bedroom house was difficult enough. When I arrived in 1950, things got even more crowded. The kitchen was so small that the person sitting in the kitchen chair nearest to the refrigerator would have to stand up if someone had to grab the milk. Laura and Jay shared a bedroom, and my crib was sandwiched into my parents' bedroom. The tiny living room had a couch, two chairs, my playpen, toys, books, and, in time, an ugly piano that was one of my sister's best gifts.

Potsdam was home to the state college, which included the Crane School of Music. This provided many musical opportunities to the community. Laura walked past Crane on her way home from school every day and heard the students practicing their instruments. Intrigued and inspired, she asked my parents for a piano. After proving herself by taking lessons using the neighbor's rickety spinet, she got her wish. My maternal grandparents purchased for her an old upright painted a hideous butterscotch orange that barely fit into the already full living room. The tiny house often reverberated with music, especially when friends gathered around the piano. Uncle Eli, who could not read music, played any requested song by ear, so he often was on the piano bench.

In 1952, my father took a job in Keeseville, New York, managing a Pearl's department store, one of several in a chain owned by my great-uncle Paul. In order to save money, my parents hired a couple of men from Pearl's to pack up the household belongings into the company truck and safely deliver them to our new home. Unfortunately, the men dropped the piano while unloading it. The instrument, never in tune to start, was now hopelessly flat with a few more non-functional keys. That didn't stop us from playing. My older siblings and I took lessons with varying degrees of mediocrity. We mixed our John Thompson piano lesson books with more popular sheet music, including such Fifties hits as "Stranger on the Shore"

"

and "Mack the Knife." Laura's and my favorites were from the American Songbook. We had a healthy collection of Rodgers and Hammerstein, Cole Porter, and George Gershwin.

By the age of twelve, I had gone through a couple of piano teachers, one who retired and one who moved away. Despite the lack of lessons, innate talent, and a decent instrument, I still loved to play. I began lobbying for a new piano. I knew, however, that getting even another second-hand one that was in a little better shape than our orange relic was probably out of financial reach for our family.

One evening before Chanukah in 1962, my parents called me into the kitchen. That afternoon, my father learned that one of his customers was moving to a smaller home and was selling a used baby grand for only five hundred dollars. Was my father interested? Yes, he was, and I was getting my wish. I cried for joy, even more so when the beautiful instrument with its shiny mahogany finish was delivered later that week. Unlike our tiny box of a house in Potsdam, our Victorian house in Keeseville had enough room for the baby grand. With a minimal rearrangement of furniture, the piano became the centerpiece of our living room.

That January, I started lessons with the young new Keeseville Central School music teacher. Initially, I was humiliated to find out that I needed to start from the beginning level books to improve my skills. Over the next three years, I managed to work my way through the third level of the John Thompson series. My teacher, knowing my love for the movie and Broadway show tunes, also supplemented the classics with more contemporary selections such as "Sunrise, Sunset" from *Fiddler on the Roof,* "You'll Never Walk Alone" from *Carousel,* and, my favorite, "Moon River."

The piano again became a gathering place for family and friends. I often played while my sisters sang along. My brother even joined in with his trombone. I missed lots of the notes, my sisters were not known for their vocal talents, and my brother was no Trombone Shorty, but we loved the chance to be together. My Grandpa Joe played Yiddish songs after he moved in with us after my grandmother's passing in 1966. Uncle Eli got to hammer out his share of songs when he visited us from Potsdam.

Marilyn at her baby grand piano circa 1971

Once I left for college, I played infrequently, mostly on school breaks. When my parents moved out of their big house in Keeseville in 1982, the piano was sold as none of the children had room for it in their homes. Before my parents downsized, I collected all the sheet music from the house and stored it in our home "just in case" we ever got a piano.

After my daughter Julie was born, I was home with two small children. The days were getting long. Knowing how much I loved my baby grand in Keeseville, Larry encouraged me to look for a piano that would fit into our home. The Yamaha upright I selected from Clark Music in Latham was delivered two weeks before my thirty-second birthday.

Marilyn and her granddaughter 2018

I now put to use the sheet music my family and I had accumulated since my sister started lessons in Potsdam many years before. I spent many hours playing the piano, both for enjoyment and for the peace and serenity it gave me.

For a short time, our son Adam took piano lessons from Brenda, a neighbor a stone's throw from our house. I don't remember his practicing, but I do remember the day he lost the $10 I had given him to pay for the lesson during the two-minute walk to Brenda's house. He decided not to continue soon after that incident.

When she was a junior in high school, Julie decided to take piano lessons for the first time. I felt my musical life had come full circle when my daughter's teacher recommended we purchase new, unmarked John Thompson lesson books. At her first and only piano recital, Julie chose Pachelbel's Canon and my old favorite, "Moon River."

When Larry and I decided to move, I initially thought of selling the piano. I rationalized that it was too expensive to ship to Florida; I didn't play *that* often; I could always use the piano in the community center a mile from our house. It was Larry who insisted that we pay the moving company to bring the piano with the rest of our household. There was no repeat of the Potsdam debacle. The piano arrived safely in our new home. From the moment I first touched the keys, I knew that we had made the right decision to move the Yamaha into our new home.

The first year we moved in, my sister Bobbie and her husband Emil came to visit. One night after dinner, I turned on the piano light and dug out some sheet music. For the next hour, we belted out songs from *Les Mis* and *Wicked* as well as our old favorites, "Sunrise, Sunset" and "Moon River." Thanks to the piano, Bobbie and I were transported back to our living room in Keeseville, me on the baby grand and Bobbie singing along. We both had tears running down our cheeks from happiness.

There Goes My Heart

The first week of September in Upstate New York is a time for new clothes, sharpened pencils, and bright yellow buses that reappear on neighborhood streets like clockwork two days after Labor Day. School opening is an important time for the children. It is also a bittersweet moment for the adults who are saying good-bye to them.

My first vivid memory was *my* first day of school. My mother walked me up the hill to the big brick building that housed all the grades for Keeseville Central. I quietly sat at a table stringing colored beads in Mrs. Ford's kindergarten classroom. My mother wordlessly slipped out the door. I didn't cry.

I was supposed to be the last of my parents' three children going off to school, but that plan failed. My sister was born three months before I entered kindergarten. Bobbie was a shining example of the little "surprise" many pre-birth-control women in their mid to late thirties experienced just when they thought diapers and formula were behind them. I am not sure if my mother pushed Bobbie in the carriage into the classroom that morning. I *am* sure dropping me off only to return to a house still equipped with a crib, a highchair, and a playpen was an ironic moment in my mother's life.

When it came time to send my son Adam off to kindergarten, I had mixed feelings. I was happy for him to be starting on his next adventure, but my mind was filled with concerns. Would his teacher, who had a reputation for being strict, be kind to my son? Would he overcome his shyness, make new

Marilyn and Julie see Adam off to school.

121

friends? My fears were certainly not alleviated when within the first week he didn't come up our driveway after the school bus pulled away. My phone call to the school triggered an alert to the driver, who found Adam fast asleep in the back the bus.

Somehow, he *did* survive his first year. Life before school became a distant memory as Julie followed Adam up the school bus steps three years later. What was so much more difficult for me was sending Adam off to college. The summer before, I shopped for comforters and dorm sized sheets and enough shampoo and soap to last for four years. The thought of his leaving the house and our no longer having four at the dinner table caused me to tear up all summer. A week before he was to leave, I was cutting up several pounds of chicken breast when I burst into tears. "I will never have to make this much chicken again!" I sobbed out loud to an empty kitchen.

The night before we drove him to the University of Rochester, most of the purchases were still in bags with the tags still on them. Unlike me who needed to be packed and ready days in advance, Adam was happy to just stuff things into suitcases and plastic bins at the last minute.

The four of us lugged his life in Rubbermaid containers up the five flights of stairs—why did my children always get the top floors of their dorms?—and Adam quickly settled in. My last memory of my son that day was his leaning back on his chair in front of his desk, proclaiming "I am going to like it here!"

Once Larry, Julie, and I got back into the car for our trip home, I felt such deep pain that I thought someone had wrenched my heart out of my body. I cried from Rochester to Syracuse. I finally stopped when Julie commented sarcastically from her perch in the back seat, "You have another child, you know!"

Sending Julie off to Williams College three years later was a little easier—maybe because she was the second child; maybe because she was only forty-five minutes away. We dropped her off in Williamstown, Massachusetts, and got her situated in her top floor—of course!—dorm room. By the time we pulled into our driveway, we were giddy with excitement over our new-found freedom. We knew that both children were happy in their college environments. That knowledge, coupled with the realization that we no longer had to worry about the daily angst of their high school lives—homework, carpools, dates for a dance—made the transition into our now empty nest smoother.

Still, each time our children came home, I found their inevitable departure difficult. After sending Julie off to college for her final year, I asked my mother if she ever got used to saying goodbye. "Oh, Marilyn," she said. "It never gets easier! Every time any one of you gets into the car and drives away, I think to myself, 'There goes my heart!'"

So, each year on the first day of school, when I see the school bus filled with children with their new clothes, their sharpened pencils their bright back packs, I will be thinking of my first day, my children's first days, and my aching heart.

My Sister Laura, The "Special" Special Ed Teacher

As a child, I was in awe of my big sister. Eight years my senior, Laura wore the best clothes (big skirts with tons of crinolines); listened to the best songs (No to Elvis; Yes to Pat Boone and Johnny Mathis); and exuded a confidence that I lacked. It wasn't until I was an adult, working with Special Olympic athletes, that I gained a greater appreciation for her true gift—her career as a special education teacher. Through the efforts of pioneers like Laura Cohen Appel, the world has become more inclusive and more understanding.

In 1958, Laura, a junior at Keeseville Central High School in upstate New York, was thinking about her future. She knew that she wanted to become a teacher, but she didn't want to teach "regular" kids. Somehow, she knew that she wanted to work with what was then called "the mentally retarded."

Every April, selected eleventh and twelfth grade students were given the opportunity to participate in "Student Teacher Day." Laura requested to be placed with Alice Benoit, who taught a life-skill class for low functioning students. That experience and further conversations with Mrs. Benoit confirmed her career choice.

On the recommendation of Dan Meagan, the guidance counselor, Laura applied to Geneseo State, a small college located in the Finger Lakes region, and only one of two in the state system offering a degree in special education.

In addition, Geneseo was progressive. According to *SUNY Geneseo: From Normal School to Public Ivy, 1871-2007,* James V. Sturges, the principal of the Geneseo Normal School, created a special education program as early as 1922. A 1920 act of the New York State Legislature stated that "[e]very school with ten or more 'subnormal' or 'unusually retarded' children was to provide a specially prepared teacher." As a result, Sturges included special education in his teacher training curriculum.

Reflecting his generation's "unease" with the stigma of "special needs" children, our father Bill Cohen was uncomfortable about her decision. "Why do you want to teach *those* students?" he questioned," Why don't you just want to be a teacher of *regular* students?" Interestingly, our father later served on the local school board for many years, and he was a proponent of special education programs, thanks in part to his daughter's work in that field.

While Laura was a junior in college, President John F. Kennedy, whose sister Rosemary had intellectual disabilities, created the President's Panel on Mental Retardation, which heralded the beginning of federal involvement and fiscal aid to states. His sister, Eunice Shriver, founded Special Olympics in honor of Rosemary, who had been hidden away from the world by her parents in private schools and, after a lobotomy to "fix her," in an institution for the remainder of her life.

Spring semester of her senior year, Laura was assigned to do her student teaching in Rochester, New York. Her first assignment was in a fourth grade "regular" classroom, an experience so horrible that Laura almost quit. My parents insisted she stick it out. Her second assignment in a special education class with a wonderful teacher and mentor again confirmed her career choice.

After she graduated in 1964, Laura took a job in Spring Valley, New York. During that first year of her teaching, special education classes were not held in a regular school building. Instead, Laura taught classes in an activities building for a nearby summer camp. A second building held the classes for the physically handicapped as well as a food service program that made student and faculty lunches every day.

Laura and her fellow teachers, left very much on their own, made the decision to divide the classes not by ages but by abilities, thereby allowing children with similar skills to progress together. For some children, education focused on basic life skills—eating, dressing, and bathing, as well as other daily living skills like shopping, banking, phone use and housekeeping. Others showing greater ability were taught skills that were part of a more standard curriculum, including reading, math, history, and science.

Teaching special education was a whole new world. Before 1961, the United States did not publicly educate any children with any disabilities. If a child had cognitive or emotional disabilities, deafness, blindness or needed speech therapy, parents had to educate their children at home or pay for private education. Parents began the process of securing public education by creating advocacy groups for their children. They met with teachers and politicians. It was not until 1965, when Laura was in her first year of

Laura Appel with Will Kocsovsky,
her significant other

teaching, that President Lyndon B. Johnson began signing off on acts designed to expand public education and its funding purposes.

Laura continued teaching special education in New York and, after her marriage, in Connecticut. In 1971, she left the classroom to become a stay-at-home mom. Five years later, the family relocated to Phoenixville, Pennsylvania, a suburb of Philadelphia.

Changes, meanwhile, were happening in special education As late as 1970, United States schools educated only one in five children with disabilities, and many states had laws excluding certain students, including children who were deaf, blind, emotionally disturbed, or "mentally retarded." In 1975, however, with the passage of the Education for All Handicapped Children Act, the United States voted to ensure that all children, regardless of their differences, should have access to free public-school education. This act helped bring federal funds into schools to help them create special education for children who did not learn the same way as general education students. The law also gave parents a right to have more of a say in their child's education. The passage of the law opened the gates for more emphasis on special education.

In 1978, with both of her children in school full-time, Laura began teaching special education in the Phoenixville Area School District, first in the regional educational service agency and eventually in the middle school as a seventh-grade resource room teacher.

Embracing new findings that special needs students did better when mainstreamed into classes with non-disabled students, Laura worked tirelessly with teachers in her team and the administration to transition the students from her stand-alone classroom to general education classrooms during specific time periods based on their skills.

Laura said that children still experienced prejudice not only from the "regular" students but also from some of the old-school educators who believed that 'retarded' children didn't belong in their classrooms. As the years progressed, however, Laura was encouraged to see teachers fully embrace the idea of inclusion.

The Education of All Handicapped Children Act continually underwent change and grew into the more expansive Individuals with Disabilities Education Act of 2004. This has become the model of public education that continues today. By the time Laura retired in 2006, most children with intellectual disabilities had been placed in inclusive classrooms where children of all abilities could learn from and with each other. "As a result," said Laura, "students with special needs feel much less stigma for being in a learning support class."

The United States has come a long way from locking away students with special needs into institutions, private schools, and isolated classrooms. "I feel a great sense of pride that I was part of the generation of educators who helped take students with intellectual disabilities out of the closets, institutions, and isolated classrooms, and put them alongside their non-disabled peers," Laura said.

These changes have fostered greater understanding, tolerance, and compassion, not only in the classroom, but also in our greater society. As we start a new school year, we owe a big thanks my big sister Laura and all the other advocates for those with special needs for their efforts.

My Brother Jay: Family Historian and Keeper of the Family Tree

Before *23andme.com* DNA kits, before genetic testing, before people poured through old census and courthouse records, our family had the best tool to connect with our ancestors—our parents, Fran and Bill Cohen.

Bill Cohen claimed he could sniff out family from ten feet or from 200 years away. According to Dad, we were related to Sir Moses Montefiore, a nineteenth-century British financier and philanthropist; Stubby Kaye, American actor and comedian most famous for his role as Nicely Nicely Johnson in *Guys and Dolls;* and Madeline Kunin, the former governor of Vermont.

Dad didn't regard fame as the only criteria to be considered *mishpachah* (Yiddish for a Jewish family or social unit including close and distant relatives). If one had any Jewish connection, Dad would find some link no matter how obscure and embrace them as one of our own.

While my father connected, my mother, Frances Cohen, kept a more reliable account of our family tree. Even into her nineties, my mother could share the convoluted genealogical history of our huge family. To add to the complexity, my father's grandfather married my mother's great-aunt, first cousins married first cousins; and two sisters from Vermont married two brothers from Toronto. That is not only a great deal of *mishpachah* (family) but a great deal of *mishagas* (confusion)! My brother Jay would listen for hours, jotting down rough drafts of the convoluted branches on yellow legal pads that he filed away for "later."

Jay also spent a great deal of time talking to our parents about the chain of family-run department stores that are intrinsically entwined into our family's history.

Pearl's Department Stores began in the early 1900s, when our maternal great-uncle Paul Ossovitz, unable to continue in the New York City sweat shops because of respiratory problems, was given money by his older sister Lillian to start a business in Vermont. Initially living with his uncle, Archik Perelman in Burlington, Paul peddled wares he carried on his back throughout the rural parts of Vermont and Upstate New York. He saved enough to purchase a horse and cart. As his business grew, he invited his brother Joe to join him.

Jay Cohen and his wife Leslie

Paul and Joe opened their first store in Alburg, Vermont. As people knew them as the "Perelman Boys," they chose the name of "Pearl's Department Store." To make the moniker even more accurate, they and most of the family changed their surname to Pearl. Joe briefly went back to New York City but returned as Paul began building a small dynasty of over 20 stores, employing his relatives as managers and clerks. Our father, Bill Cohen, was one of those relatives, spending most of his life managing one of Uncle Paul's stores in Keeseville, New York.

By the late 1980s, however, big box stores and highway systems like the Northway, rang the death knell for small-town family-run businesses. Pearl's closed its last store in 1988, only remembered through those that worked or shopped there and dusty records. In 2015, my brother Jay, retired and always a self-confessed lover of minutia and trivia, began researching the history of each of the stores and the families involved. He Googled the Internet for news stories, advertisements, and pictures. He contacted historians in the stores' towns. He reached out to the descendants of the relatives that managed or worked in Pearl's. He then expanded his research to include stores and businesses owned by *mishpachah* that were not connected to Pearl's, including paternal relatives and my in-laws, who owned Shapiros of Schuylerville in Upstate New York.

Jay incorporated all his findings into a website he calls A Family of Stores. "If you grew up in upstate New York (The North Country) or in northern Vermont anywhere from the 1930s through the 1980s, you probably remember a Pearl's Department Store in your hometown," Jay wrote on the site's home page (*www.afamilyofstores.com*). "You went there with your mom or your friends. You bought your Wrangler jeans and your school clothes or a Christmas gift. A Pearl's store was there before the Kmarts, Ames, and Walmarts and the Northway."

The ongoing project, which Jay calls a "labor of love," also drew on his interest in genealogy. His two sons began hounding him. "Learning about the Pearl's chain is fine," they said. "But when are you going to pull out all those yellow legal pads you have stuffed in a drawer and create a family tree for posterity?" It took a pandemic to motivate Jay to dig them out.

Early in the COVID lockdown, my three siblings and I connected with our paternal first cousins through weekly Zoom sessions. As we continued to shelter in place, our group of seven expanded to include over 22 cousins, their spouses, and even their children.

Each meeting was consumed by the question, "How are we all related?" Jay, who had screen-shared his *afamilyofstores.com* website, offered to pull it all together.

Using a template from *ancestry.com,* Mom's notes, his website, and updated information he gathered from the Zooms, Jay meticulously created the framework of a family tree that would document both paternal and maternal sides of our ever-expanding family. When finished, it will include everyone from Moses Montifiore (Dad was right, as he was about Stubby Kaye and Madeline Kunin) down to my parent's latest great-grandchild, my grandson, a span of over 200 years. Thanks to Jay's efforts, we not only know our roots but also our far-flung branches. We know Mom and Dad are smiling down from heaven, so proud that their son took on the mantle of the family historian and keeper of the family tree.

Initially, we all were hesitant to submit our DNA to one of the popular ancestry sites to learn more. Two reasons. First, our entire family history goes back to the shtetl in Eastern European. Those cousins who had their tests done showed us as 98% Ashkenazi (Jews with roots in Eastern Europe). No surprises there. The second reason is that—well— we thought we had more relatives than we could handle!

Jay, however, finally bit (spit?) the bullet and sent in his saliva to two companies. He is now having a field day connecting our family tree to long lost relatives as far away as South Africa and, in the case of one second cousin, as close as one mile from his home in Florida.

As Jay says, Bring them on!" After all, we are Bill and Fran Cohen's children. And we love our family…all of them.

My Sister Bobbie: Little Miss Sunshine

Every *simcha* (celebration) is a cause for rejoicing. However, for the Cohen family, my niece's bat mitzvah in 2009 was an especially joyful occasion.

My sister Bobbie and her husband Emil started planning for their daughter Marissa's bat mitzvah soon after their rabbi had given them the December 5, 2009 date. Since everything had worked out well at their son Michael's bar mitzvah and party in 2005, they decided to have a similar service and a party at the same venue.

In May 2008, Bobbie received devastating news. While both her recent mammogram and ultrasound had come out normal, Bobbie insisted on following up with a dermatologist to biopsy a small cyst. Everyone, including her doctors, was shocked at the diagnosis: she had breast cancer.

Bobbie called me on her way home from the doctor. She sobbed; I tried to console her; she asked me to be at our parents' apartment that evening when she called them. My parents took the news especially hard. No one in our family had ever had breast cancer. How could this happen to their baby, their beautiful Bobbie? Although they were too old to help her physically, they promised that they would be there for emotional support and would pray for her recovery.

We all were sad that evening, but that was the last time I heard my little sister cry. "There is a reason that everyone calls me Little Miss Sunshine," Bobbie told me a few days later. "I refuse to be anything but positive. I will beat this." Over the next year, Bobbie underwent chemotherapy, a mastectomy, radiation, and reconstruction. The support of her husband, children, family, and friends helped her. It was Bobbie's positive attitude, however, that got all of us through the stressful time. She cheerfully went to her "chemo parties" and continued her exercise regimen. She embraced wearing wigs, declaring, "My hair now looks good all the time." A few hours after having her mastectomy, she was on the phone chatting with family and friends. "I am on a road with a few bumps and turns, but it will straighten out again," she said. "Meanwhile, I have a bat mitzvah to plan."

Bobbie and her husband Emil Chiauzzi

In the middle of Bobbie's ordeal, my father's health began to deteriorate. Just before he died, Dad received a phone call from his oldest grandson and his wife to tell him that they were expecting their first child. "It will be a boy." Dad said. "Name him after me, but call him William, not Wilfred." He passed away a day later, November 20, 2008. That left my mother dealing with Bobbie's illness and the loss of her husband of sixty-eight years. Mom was philosophical about being a widow. "Life is about change," she said. "Bill and I had a wonderful marriage, and I have to accept that he is gone." She spent quality time with her friends and family. She drew strength from both Bobbie's optimism and the positive reports from her 'baby's' cancer doctors.

By the following December, everyone was ready for the chance to celebrate. Friends and family came from New York, Arizona, Colorado, and California. The youngest guest was five-month-old William, or Will, my parents' newest great-grandchild, named after my father. Before Friday night services, we all gathered in the top floor of the hotel to enjoy a huge Italian buffet set up by Bobbie and Emil. The next morning, Marissa did a beautiful job leading the service and reading the Torah and haftorah. Bobbie, still sporting a wig, looked absolutely radiant. Emil just beamed with pride for his family, and Michael cheered on his sister. The party was a joy. My mother, not looking at all like a ninety-one-year-old widow, danced every hora and electric slide and cha-cha-cha. We took pictures of the entire Cohen family, with the four children and their spouses, the eight grandchildren, and the seven great grandchildren. I was not the only one to shed tears of joy. "We were not only celebrating Marissa's bat mitzvah," my mother later reflected. "We were also celebrating Bobbie's good health."

Fourteen months later, my mother's health declined rapidly. As she approached her last days, Bobbie drove in from Boston to be by her side. My little sister, who had never taken a medical class in her life, turned out to the best nurse in the family. Bobbie took command and guided us in tending to her needs until Mom joined her beloved Bill on March 2, 2011.

Bobbie and Emil visited us the second year we moved to Florida. Larry and I pride ourselves in our energy and stamina, but we could barely keep up with the two of them. We all explored Spaceship Earth and the World Showcase at Epcot; rode the Tower of Terror and watched fireworks at Hollywood Studios. We took pictures with 'Albert Einstein' and 'Steve Jobs' at Orlando's wax museum. And through it all, Bobbie sparkled and smiled. And I thank G-d every day that my little sister is healthy, active, and remains our Little Miss Sunshine.

I Would Do It All Again: Dealing with Aging Parents

When my parents moved up from Florida to Coburg Village in 2005, we knew they were settling into a place that offered them independence and the kind of life they wanted to lead. As it was

Bill, Fran, Jay, Marilyn, Bobbie & Laura 2007

only four miles from our home, Larry and I, as well as my siblings, had peace of mind knowing we were close enough to be there when they needed us and to watch over their physical and emotional health. At times, however, providing that oversight was not easy.

Every Sunday, Larry and I had a standing date with my parents to go out to eat at a local restaurant. Mom's favorite choice was a Chinese buffet as she loved spareribs and anything fried. Dad said he preferred Italian, although his choices in those restaurants were sometimes more McDonalds than *mangiare bene*. He once insisted on our driving to an Italian restaurant in Schenectady in the dead of winter and proceeded to order minestrone soup and chicken nuggets.

One week, on the advice of friends, we decided to take them to Verdile's, a landmark Italian restaurant in Troy. As was the custom, Larry and I picked them up in the front of their building. I helped my father get into the front passenger seat, helped my mother get into the back seat behind Dad, and took my place behind Larry. Larry put the car in gear and headed to our destination. Around two miles down the road, my father said, "Oh, damn! I forgot my teeth!"

"We'll turn around and get them," offered Larry.

"That's okay," said Dad. "I can just gum my food."

Larry ignored him and turned the car around.

When we got back to Coburg, I took my parents' keys, went through the foyer, ran up the stairs to their second-floor apartment, unlocked the door, grabbed a set of dentures out of a bowl in the bathroom, wrapped them in a paper towel, relocked the door, and headed back to the car.

"Thanks, Marilyn," said Dad, as he started putting them into his mouth. A second later, he yelled, "Hey! These aren't my teeth!"

"Oh, they must be mine!" Mom chimed in from the back seat. "I forgot them, too! Hand them back, Bill!"

As Mom was getting her bridge into her mouth, I went back to the apartment, found the second bowl with *Dad's* teeth on the bathroom vanity, and ran back to the car. Now that all the dentures were in place, we were ready to complete our trip to Verdile's.

All was fairly quiet for a couple of miles. "I read an interesting article in *Consumer Reports* this week about one of my prescription medicines," Dad piped up. "You know how I am always having to run to the bathroom? Well, that's one of the side effects of one of the damn pills I have to take."

"You have congestive heart failure, Dad," I said. "Your doctor put you on diuretics to prevent fluid from building up in your lungs. You've landed in the Ellis Hospital emergency room three times since you moved here when you failed to take them."

"Well, the heck with all these doctors!" said Dad. "I am tired of constantly having to pee. I've decided to stop taking them. Haven't swallowed any of those suckers for four days!"

I immediately conjured up in my mind another ambulance ride for Dad and another lost day of work for me. Meanwhile, I thought Larry was going to drive off the road.

Mom patted my hand and whispered to me, "I'll take care of this, sweetheart. Don't worry." By the time we got to the restaurant, all four of us were on edge, hungry, and ready for a good dinner. Fortunately, Verdile's lived up to its reputation. Our pasta-based meals were delicious, and the staff was friendly, kind and accommodating. Judging from the demographics of the people sitting around the room, the staff in the restaurant was obviously used to serving senior citizens.

As our waiter cleared the table before he brought coffee, my mother popped out her bridge and wrapped it in a napkin. Although I was used to this in our own homes, I was a little grossed out that she was doing it in public. I also worried she'd lose the bridge—an expensive proposition.

I started to stammer an explanation and warning to the waiter. "Err…please don't take the napkin. My mother's teeth are in it."

He broke out in a big smile. "Don't worry! We're used to that here. Can't tell you how many times we've had to do a dumpster dive for a set of false teeth or a hearing aid!"

We drank our coffee, paid the bill, and drove my parents back to Coburg Village. The next day, I called my mother, and she assured me that Dad was back on his water pills.

"Thanks for dinner, Marilyn," Mom said. "Dad and I really enjoyed our afternoon with the two of you. We'll have to come up with another fun place to eat next Sunday."

"Sure, Mom," I said aloud. "Let's do that!" In my mind, however, I was thinking, 'Let's just make it less exciting.'

The four of us enjoyed many more Sunday outings until my father's passing in November 2008. Larry and I kept up the tradition with my mother until her death in March 2011. To this day, despite the misplaced teeth, the medical revelations, and the not-so-healthy Chinese buffets, we fondly remember those Sunday dinners we shared with Mom and Dad.

Does History Repeat Itself?

In 2015, Larry and I sold our home in Upstate New York and relocated to a community in Central Florida. As Larry and I have fully embraced our new life in the Sunshine State, it is interesting to compare our retirement life near Orlando to my parents' retirement years near Fort Lauderdale.

When the last of the Cohen children headed for college, my parents spent a couple of weeks each winter in Florida. When they retired, they sold the house in Keeseville and moved into their cottage on Lake Champlain. They escaped to Florida for two or three months in the dead of winter, splitting their time between short-term rentals and relatives' pull-out couches. In time, they purchased a one-bedroom condo in Hawaiian Gardens, a complex in Lauderdale Lakes that they had heard about through a friend who lived at the complex.

After years of living in a community with lots of snow and with few Jewish people, they thrived in the sunshine and in the company of *Yiddishkeit*, fellow Jews who had moved to the Sunshine State from New York City and Long Island. Their lives fell into a pattern. They shopped at Publix and went to their doctors' appointments in the morning. By noon, they joined all the other retirees by the small community pool. The women splashed around in the water while the men kibitzed on their beach chairs under large umbrellas. The conversation consisted of bad jokes, condo gossip, politics, and discussions as to which restaurants offered the best early bird specials. My mother had grown up speaking Yiddish to her parents, and my father knew a few expressions, so they started a popular Yiddish Club that met once a week. Dad played poker; Mom went to flea markets with friends.

Outside of my father's occasional game of golf, my parents got their exercise walking back and forth to the pool. Deerfield Beach was only a half an hour away, but my father hated the sun, the heat, and the sand. As a result, my mother, who didn't drive in Florida, limited her visits to the ocean to when her children could take her when we visited.

Hawaiian Gardens offered entertainment in the clubhouse, usually a singer or a comedian who had worked on the Borscht Belt. The performers weren't paid a great deal, many were a little beyond their prime, and the audience could be downright cruel. During one of our visits, a woman singer was belting out Broadway tunes. When she asked if the audience would like her to do an encore, one of the residents yelled out, "No! You're terrible! Get off the stage!"

Larry and I flew down at least once a year and joined them in their routine. In the morning, I would take my mother to the supermarket or the flea market. At noon, we headed to the pool. At three o'clock, no matter how beautiful the weather, we all went upstairs to get ready to leave their apartment by four o'clock for that day's early bird special. The meals varied in quality, but there were tons of food with enough leftovers, extra bread, lemon slices, and a few Sweet 'n Low packets to take home for the next day's lunch. Even when they relocated to a larger condo, their routine remained the same. And their lives always included visits from relatives and friends from New York as well as get-togethers with new friends they had made.

Although we enjoyed our visits, Larry and I could not picture ourselves living the sedentary East Coast Florida condo life that my parents enjoyed. When we moved to our adult active community in Central Florida, we felt we had found our own slice of heaven. Our home sat on a large scenic lot with plenty of room for family and friends to visit. Our community had two community recreational centers where I could take exercise classes and swim laps. Larry could play pickleball. We had miles of neighborhood streets where we could take long walks and longer bike rides. Many clubs and groups offered us innumerable ways to meet people from around the country and the world. Many of the activities revolved around the synagogue and the Shalom Club, but we also participated in club activities offered by groups with ties to Italy, England, the Caribbean, and Western Upstate New York. We had a full, diverse life.

Once we lived here for a few months, however, I realized how much we have in common with my parents. Has it been that different? We head to the pickleball courts, the pool, and fitness classes in the morning. Then we plan our doctors' appointments and our trip to Publix in the afternoon. Flipped schedule, but.... We often head to our favorite restaurant by four o'clock so we can beat the crowds. Recent entertainment included a headliner from the Sixties whose toupee and fancy tux didn't cover the fact that his body and voice were not what they were fifty years ago. The ocean is only ninety minutes away, but we don't feel like fighting the traffic. We share a great deal of time with our family and our old friends from around the country. And, like my parents, we escape the summer heat by spending time in Frisco, Colorado. It's not Lake Champlain, but at 9100 feet it certainly beats Florida's summers.

Larry & Marilyn escape the Florida heat in Colorado

Both of our children have visited us in our home in Florida. They and their families have repeatedly told us they were glad that we are so happy here. However, I doubt if either of them or their families would select the lifestyle we have chosen. Our daughter Julie and her husband Sam love living in the Rockies, where they have mountains, forests, and plenty of trails available for hiking and skiing. Our son Adam and his wife love living in San Francisco, enjoying all that wonderful city and California have to offer. I hope wherever my children live, they will enjoy sunny skies, good health, and lots of activities to keep busy. Most importantly, I hope they find joy in wherever life takes them.

In her eulogy to Grandma Fran, Julie spoke of my mother's legacy. "She taught me about the woman I'd like to be, one filled with love, generosity, wisdom, wit, empathy, and a belief that we can create our own happiness in life by searching for the blessings." That is the life my mother, "Frances Fradel" Cohen, lived with her "Dear Bill." May their memories—and the memories they shared with all who knew and loved them—be a blessing.

Fighting COVID Fatigue
with Family Memories

Passover did not completely pass over us the second year of the pandemic. When the major Jewish holiday occurred the previous spring, we were only three weeks into the reality of COVID-19. Larry and I had a small, quiet, seder for two. Twelve months later, we knew we were at least having a virtual Zoom seder with our Kissimmee, Florida, synagogue.

My husband Larry and I felt very fortunate. As were our Hebrew ancestors, our family and circle of friends had been spared the "angel of death" in that we lost no one to this (God willing) once-in-a-lifetime scourge. Friends who contracted the illness had survived, albeit with some lingering effects that we hoped and prayed will result in a *r'fuah sh'leimah*, a complete recovery.

Despite my gratitude, too many times while sheltering in place, I felt that more than Passover had passed us by. I knew I shared the feelings of so many others: that we had lost a year of our lives. It had not only been the life events—first birthday parties, bar mitzvahs, weddings, graduations, even funerals. It had also been the small things: a restaurant dinner with friends; a movie or play; a live sporting event; a simple hug from a friend.

This feeling of ennui especially hit me when February arrived. When we lived in Upstate New York, the second month of the year had always been difficult, as I was tired of the cold, the snow, the bleakness of winter. Now that we were living in Florida, we were liberated from the end-of-winter blues. Larry and I still were able to enjoy long walks and long bike rides in the sunshine. Physically, I was doing fine. But emotionally, I felt sad and cold and dark. Would this pandemic ever end? Would our children and grandchildren be able to get vaccinated? Would we be able to travel to see them this summer? When will the world return to normal?

Getting on Zoom calls was a chore; if I did sign on, I remained quiet, content to work on my crewel piece or check my text messages. Telephone calls were even more difficult; it was just too much work to talk about our endless Groundhog Day routine: morning exercise; afternoon puzzles and projects; late afternoon dinners; and evenings on the couch watching Netflix or reading a book.

In the middle of all this, I was working on my third book. When completed, **Fradel's Stories** would be a compilation of essays my mother had written in the last five years of her long life as well as essays I had written about my parents and family, many of which have been published in the (Capital Region, New York) *Jewish World.* My mother had passed away on March 2, 2011, and I was determined to get the first "run" to my editor to correspond with the tenth anniversary of her death. I devoted hours to organizing, editing, and re-editing. What should have been a labor of love was turning into just labor. Of course, that put more pressure on me, something that I certainly didn't need in my emotionally depleted state.

On the third Saturday in February, I opted out of my usual exercise-in-the-morning routine and continued editing the second hard copy of the manuscript. When I got to the chapter that Mom had called My Romances, I brightened. "The saying goes, 'You have to kiss many frogs until you meet your true love,'" my mom had written in one of my favorite stories. "Well, I knew many frogs." She then went on to describe the men she dated while living with her parents and working in New York City until she was introduced to Bill Cohen, her brother and her cousin's co-worker in an Upstate New York clothing store.

After a whirlwind three-month courtship, my father proposed over ice cream on February 14, 1940. "We had just seen Gone With the Wind," Mom wrote. "Bill must have thought I was Scarlett O'Hara, and I must have thought he was Rhett Butler." They were engaged!

Separated by over 300 miles, they conducted a long-distance romance. Over the next six months, they saw each other infrequently but wrote each other often. Mom had kept the letters in her dresser her entire life. "Where are they now?" I wondered. Then I remembered that I had found them when my siblings and I were emptying her apartment soon after her funeral. They were in a metal box that held all my treasured correspondences.

Even though I had known about my parents' love letters for at least sixty years, I had never actually read them until that Saturday morning. The first one I read, from my father, spoke of feeling "sad and cold and dark." Oh, my goodness! He was describing me! His remaining letters expressed his love and excitement about their pending marriage. My mom's letters shared some of his romantic sentiments, but most of them described wedding preparations and constant reminders for Bill to get his Wassermann test before the August 20 ceremony.

After reading them all, I called my three siblings to share the emotional news of my find. That triggered more memories, more family stories. Laura reminisced how her eight-year-old self had found our parents' love letters and decided to play post office by delivering them to each of the mailboxes on our street in Potsdam. Jay remembered how, while living in that same Upstate New York house, he and a fellow five-year-old had called the fire department to report a "blaze" so the two of them could get a firsthand look at the town's new fire engine. Bobbie remembered another letter—the one my parents had written to her in 1977 when, as a recent college graduate, she was struggling to find a job—that she still has over 43 years later.

After my phone calls, I went back to the kitchen table to resume work on my book, but I was no longer alone. My siblings' stories echoed in my mind. More strikingly, I felt my parents' strong presence surrounding me with encouragement to keep writing and with quiet assurance that "this too shall pass." Recalling through their stories how they had survived the Spanish Flu, the Great Depression, World War II, and their own nine decades of ups and downs, I knew my family and I would survive COVID-19 and its resulting *tsouris*—troubles.

Ten days later, I felt confident enough to send my manuscript to my editor. We still had months of work ahead—more editing, picture placements, cover design. But I knew that by September 1, 2021, what would have been my mother's 104th birthday, **Fradel's Stories** would be launched on Amazon.

Revived, I gave my house a thorough cleaning, made my chicken soup and matzoh balls, chopped my apples and nuts for the *charotzes*, set our table for our Zoom seder. With all the recent good news of the medical front, I had faith that next year's seder would be a more crowded, joyous, affair. Meanwhile, Passover and spring were here. Thanks to the love and memories my parents and siblings had shared with me, I no longer was sad and cold and dark. I was happy and warm and filled with light.

Enjoy this assortment of Cohen Family photos!

Fran and Bill's legacy lives on
in their grandchildren and great-grandchildren!

141

About the Authors

FRANCES "FRADEL" COHEN, the daughter of two Lithuanian Jewish immigrants, was born in Harlem in 1917 and grew up in a Jewish neighborhood in Coney Island. When she married Wilfred "Bill" Cohen in 1940, she moved with him over three hundred miles to Upstate New York. Four moves resulted in four children, so they stopped moving. After their youngest child was born, Fran took on more and more responsibility helping Bill manage Pearl's Department Store in Keeseville, New York, and starting in 1966, three Village Bazaars in Keeseville, Rouses Point, and Port Henry. After their retirement, they split their time between their beloved cottage on Lake Champlain and a condo in Southeast Florida. Their lasting legacy includes their four children, eight grandchildren, nine great-grandchildren, and an extended web of family and friends who loved them and their stories.

MARILYN COHEN SHAPIRO grew up in a very close-knit family in a small town on Lake Champlain in upstate New York. Since retiring from a career in adult education and relocating from Saratoga County to Florida, she is now writing down family stories she has thought about during her entire life. She and her husband Larry are proud to have raised two children who enjoy reading, learning, and traveling as much as they do. Marilyn loves singing along to Broadway musicals, getting lost on well-marked trails in national parks, and eating vanilla ice cream. Marilyn has been a regular contributor to the bi-weekly publication, *The Jewish World* (Capital Region, New York), since 2013. Her articles have also been published in *Heritage Florida Jewish News* and several websites including the *Union of Reform Judaism, Jewish War Veterans of the United States of America, Growing Bolder, and Jewish Women of Words (Australia)*. She is the author of two previous compilations of her stories, **There Goes My Heart** (2016) and **Tikkun Olam: Stories of Repairing an Unkind World.** (2018). Both books are available in paperback and e-book format on Amazon.

Her blog is www.theregoesmyheart.me.
You may email her at shapcomp18@gmail.com.

Photo Credits

All photos in this book not credited were provided by Marilyn Cohen Shapiro, the author. *In no way does use of the photos below suggest that the licensors endorse the author or her book.*

P.20 Coney Island. Courtesy Wikimedia Commons: Coney Island Cyclone New York September 2016 003.jpg

P.24 Thanksgiving. Courtesy Wikipedia Commons: THANKSGIVING DAY DINNER (held by) HOTEL MARLBOROUGH (at) NY (HOTEL) (NYPL Hades-270314-474964).jpg

P.47 American Flag. Thanks to Adam Birkett @abrkett for making this photo available freely on Unsplash. https://unsplash.com/photos/Zf4NoRKEhtE

P.49 Sadie Thompson. Courtesy of Wikimedia Commons. Sadie_Thompson_poster.jpg

P.62 Palms. https://upload.wikimedia.org/wikipedia/commons/2/2c/ Palm_Trees_in_Deerfield_Beach%2C_Florida.jpg

P.65 Coburg Village. Courtesy of Pam Welch, Marketing and Public Relations Coburg Village, Rexford, NY

P.69 Rings. Public Domain. "https://commons.wikimedia.org/w/index.php?curid=584489">Link</a>

P.70 Awards. Photo by Clipart Panda http://www.clipartpanda.com/clipart_images/dubose-63692612

P.76 Confidence. You've Got This. Photo by Sydney rae on Unsplash. https://unsplash.com/photos/geM5lzDj4Iw

P.77 Eleanor Roosevelt. Public Domain https://commons.wikimedia.org/w/index.php?search=eleanor+roosevelt&title=Spe cial:MediaSearch&go=Go&type=image

P.78 Ice box. https://commons.wikimedia.org/wiki/File:1920s_ice_box_ using_ice_blocks_to_keep_food_cold.jpg

P.89 Kreplach. https://www.dreamstime.com/royalty-free-stock-image-kreplach-jewish-ravioli-chicken-soup-image14539146. https://www.dreamstime.com/photos-images/kreplach.html?pg=2

P.103 Keeseville Free Library. Courtesy of Keeseville Free Library on their Facebook page. 13327356_1602881096690806_675665799999995914

P.130 Clothesline. By Michael Jastremski - OpenPhoto.net, CC BY-SA 2.5, https://commons.wikimedia.org/w/index.php?curid=670423